PRENTICE-HALL FOUNDATIONS OF PHILOSOPHY SERIES

D0439760

Virgil Aldrich	PHILOSOPHY OF ART
William Alston	PHILOSOPHY OF LANGUAGE
Stephen Barker	PHILOSOPHY OF MATHEMATICS
Roderick Chisholm	THEORY OF KNOWLEDGE
William Dray	PHILOSOPHY OF HISTORY
Joel Feinberg	POLITICAL PHILOSOPHY
William Frankena	ETHICS
Martin Golding	PHILOSOPHY OF LAW
Carl Hempel	PHILOSOPHY OF NATURAL SCIENCE
John Hick	PHILOSOPHY OF RELIGION
John Lenz	PHILOSOPHY OF EDUCATION
Richard Rudner	PHILOSOPHY OF SOCIAL SCIENCE
Wesley Salmon	LOGIC
Jerome Shaffer	PHILOSOPHY OF MIND
Richard Taylor	METAPHYSICS

Elizabeth and Monroe Beardsley, editors

PHILOSOPHY

OF

NATURAL

SCIENCE

FOUNDATIONS OF PHILOSOPHY SERIES

Carl G. Hempel

Princeton University

PRENTICE-HALL, INC.   ENGLEWOOD CLIFFS, N. J.

PHILOSOPHY OF NATURAL SCIENCE, Hempel

FOUNDATIONS OF PHILOSOPHY SERIES

C-66382

Current printing (last digit):
17   16

PRENTICE-HALL   INTERNATIONAL,   INC.,   London

PRENTICE-HALL   OF   AUSTRALIA,   PTY.   LTD.,   Sydney

PRENTICE-HALL   OF   CANADA,   LTD.,   Toronto

PRENTICE-HALL OF INDIA (PRIVATE) LTD., New Delhi

PRENTICE-HALL   OF   JAPAN,   INC.,   Tokyo

FOUNDATIONS

OF PHILOSOPHY

Many of the problems of philosophy are of such broad relevance to human concerns, and so complex in their ramifications, that they are, in one form or another, perennially present. Though in the course of time they yield in part to philosophical inquiry, they may need to be rethought by each age in the light of its broader scientific knowledge and deepened ethical and religious experience. Better solutions are found by more refined and rigorous methods. Thus, one who approaches the study of philosophy in the hope of understanding the best of what it affords will look for both fundamental issues and contemporary achievements.

Written by a group of distinguished philosophers, the Foundations of Philosophy Series aims to exhibit some of the main problems in the various fields of philosophy as they stand at the present stage of philosophical history.

While certain fields are likely to be represented in most introductory courses in philosophy, college classes differ widely in emphasis, in method of instruction, and in rate of progress. Every instructor needs freedom to change his course as his own philosophical interests, the size and makeup of his classes, and the needs of his students vary from year to year. The fifteen volumes in the Foundations of Philosophy Series—each complete in itself, but complementing the others—offer a new flexibility to the instructor, who can create his own textbook by combining several volumes as he wishes, and can choose different combinations at different times. Those volumes that are not used in an introductory course will be found valuable, along with other texts or collections of readings, for the more specialized upper-level courses.

ELIZABETH BEARDSLEY   MONROE BEARDSLEY

To

Peter Andrew

and

Toby Anne

PREFACE

This book offers an introduction to some of the central topics in the contemporary methodology and philosophy of natural science. In order to meet the exigencies of the available space, I decided to deal with a limited number of important issues in some detail rather than to attempt a sketchy survey of a wider range of subjects. Although the book is elementary in character, I have sought to avoid misleading oversimplification, and I have pointed out several unresolved issues that are among the subjects of current research and discussion.

Readers who wish to explore more fully the questions here examined or to acquaint themselves with other problem areas in the philosophy of science will find suggestions for further reading in the brief bibliography at the end of this volume.

A substantial part of this book was written in 1964, during the last months of a year I spent as a Fellow of the Center for Advanced Study in the Behavioral Sciences. I am happy to express my appreciation for that opportunity.

Finally, I extend warm thanks to the editors of this series, Elizabeth and Monroe Beardsley, for their valuable advice, and to Jerome B. Neu for his efficient help in reading the proofs and preparing the index.

CARL G. HEMPEL

CONTENTS

Philosophy of Natural Science

SCOPE AND AIM

OF THIS BOOK

1

The different branches of scientific inquiry may be divided into two major groups: the empirical and the nonempirical sciences. The former seek to explore, to describe, to explain, and to predict the occurrences in the world we live in. Their statements, therefore, must be checked against the facts of our experience, and they are acceptable only if they are properly supported by empirical evidence. Such evidence is obtained in many different ways: by experimentation, by systematic observation, by interviews or surveys, by psychological or clinical testing, by careful examination of documents, inscriptions, coins, archeological relics, and so forth. This dependence on empirical evidence distinguishes the empirical sciences from the nonempirical disciplines of logic and pure mathematics, whose propositions are proved without essential reference to empirical findings.

The empirical sciences in turn are often divided into the natural sciences and the social sciences. The criterion for this division is much less clear than that which distinguishes empirical from nonempirical inquiry, and there is no general agreement on precisely where the dividing line is to be drawn. Usually, the natural sciences are understood to include physics, chemistry, biology, and their border areas; the social sciences are taken to comprise sociology, political science, anthropology, economics, historiography, and related disciplines. Psychology is sometimes assigned to one field, sometimes to the other, and not infrequently it is said to overlap both.

In the present series of books, the philosophy of the natural sciences and the philosophy of the social sciences are dealt with in different volumes. This separation of topics is to serve the practical purpose of permitting a more adequate discussion of the large field of the philosophy of science; it is not intended to prejudge the question whether the division is also of systematic significance, i.e., whether the natural sciences differ fundamentally from the social sciences in subject matter, objectives, methods, or presuppositions. That there are such basic differences between those large fields has been widely asserted, and on various interesting grounds. A thorough exploration of these claims requires a close analysis of the social sciences as well as of the natural sciences and thus goes beyond the scope of this little volume. Nevertheless, our discussion will shed some light on the issue. For from time to time in our exploration of the philosophy of the natural sciences, we will have occasion to cast a comparative glance at the social sciences, and we will see that many of our findings concerning the methods and the rationale of scientific inquiry apply to the social as well as to the natural sciences. The words 'sciences' and 'scientific' will therefore often be used to refer to the entire domain of empirical science; but when clarity demands it, qualifying phrases will be added.

The high prestige that science enjoys today is no doubt attributable in large measure to the striking successes and the rapidly expanding reach of its applications. Many branches of empirical science have come to provide a basis for associated technologies, which put the results of scientific inquiry to practical use and which in turn often furnish pure or basic research with new data, new problems, and new tools for investigation.

But apart from aiding man in his search for control over his environment, science answers another, disinterested, but no less deep and persistent, urge: namely, his desire to gain ever wider knowledge and ever deeper understanding of the world in which he finds himself. In the chapters that follow, we will consider how these principal objectives of scientific inquiry are achieved. We will examine how scientific knowledge is arrived at, how it is supported, and how it changes; we will consider how science explains empirical facts, and what kind of understanding its explanations can give us; and in the course of these discussions, we will also touch upon some more general problems concerning the presuppositions and the limits of scientific inquiry, scientific knowledge, and scientific understanding.

SCIENTIFIC INQUIRY:

INVENTION AND TEST

2

2.1 A case history as an example As a simple illustration of some important aspects of scientific inquiry let us consider Semmelweis' work on childbed fever. Ignaz Semmelweis, a physician of Hungarian birth, did this work during the years from 1844 to 1848 at the Vienna General Hospital. As a member of the medical staff of the First Maternity Division in the hospital, Semmelweis was distressed to find that a large proportion of the women who were delivered of their babies in that division contracted a serious and often fatal illness known as puerperal fever or childbed fever. In 1844, as many as 260 out of 3,157 mothers in the First Division, or 8.2 per cent, died of the disease; for 1845, the death rate was 6.8 per cent, and for 1846, it was 11.4 per cent. These figures were all the more alarming because in the adjacent Second Maternity Division of the same hospital, which accommodated almost as many women as the First, the death toll from childbed fever was much lower: 2.3, 2.0, and 2.7 per cent for the same years. In a book that he wrote later on the causation and the prevention of childbed fever, Semmelweis describes his efforts to resolve the dreadful puzzle.[1]

He began by considering various explanations that were current at the time; some of these he rejected out of hand as incompatible with well-established facts; others he subjected to specific tests.

[1] The story of Semmelweis' work and of the difficulties he encountered forms a fascinating page in the history of medicine. A detailed account, which includes translations and paraphrases of large portions of Semmelweis' writings, is given in W. J. Sinclair, *Semmelweis: His Life and His Doctrine* (Manchester, England: Manchester University Press, 1909). Brief quoted phrases in this chapter are taken from this work. The highlights of Semmelweis' career are recounted in the first chapter of P. de Kruif, *Men Against Death* (New York: Harcourt, Brace & World, Inc., 1932).

One widely accepted view attributed the ravages of puerperal fever to "epidemic influences", which were vaguely described as "atmospheric-cosmic-telluric changes" spreading over whole districts and causing childbed fever in women in confinement. But how, Semmelweis reasons, could such influences have plagued the First Division for years and yet spared the Second? And how could this view be reconciled with the fact that while the fever was raging in the hospital, hardly a case occurred in the city of Vienna or in its surroundings: a genuine epidemic, such as cholera, would not be so selective. Finally, Semmelweis notes that some of the women admitted to the First Division, living far from the hospital, had been overcome by labor on their way and had given birth in the street: yet despite these adverse conditions, the death rate from childbed fever among these cases of "street birth" was lower than the average for the First Division.

On another view, overcrowding was a cause of mortality in the First Division. But Semmelweis points out that in fact the crowding was heavier in the Second Division, partly as a result of the desperate efforts of patients to avoid assignment to the notorious First Division. He also rejects two similar conjectures that were current, by noting that there were no differences between the two Divisions in regard to diet or general care of the patients.

In 1846, a commission that had been appointed to investigate the matter attributed the prevalence of illness in the First Division to injuries resulting from rough examination by the medical students, all of whom received their obstetrical training in the First Division. Semmelweis notes in refutation of this view that (a) the injuries resulting naturally from the process of birth are much more extensive than those that might be caused by rough examination; (b) the midwives who received their training in the Second Division examined their patients in much the same manner but without the same ill effects; (c) when, in response to the commission's report, the number of medical students was halved and their examinations of the women were reduced to a minimum, the mortality, after a brief decline, rose to higher levels than ever before.

Various psychological explanations were attempted. One of them noted that the First Division was so arranged that a priest bearing the last sacrament to a dying woman had to pass through five wards before reaching the sickroom beyond: the appearance of the priest, preceded by an attendant ringing a bell, was held to have a terrifying and debilitating effect upon the patients in the wards and thus to make them more likely victims of childbed fever. In the Second Division, this adverse factor was absent, since the priest had direct access to the sickroom. Semmelweis decided to test this conjecture. He persuaded the priest to come by a roundabout route and without ringing of the bell, in order to reach the sick chamber silently and unobserved. But the mortality in the First Division did not decrease.

A new idea was suggested to Semmelweis by the observation that in the First Division the women were delivered lying on their backs; in the Second Division, on their sides. Though he thought it unlikely, he decided "like a drowning man clutching at a straw", to test whether this difference in procedure was significant. He introduced the use of the lateral position in the First Division, but again, the mortality remained unaffected.

At last, early in 1847, an accident gave Semmelweis the decisive clue for his solution of the problem. A colleague of his, Kolletschka, received a puncture wound in the finger, from the scalpel of a student with whom he was performing an autopsy, and died after an agonizing illness during which he displayed the same symptoms that Semmelweis had observed in the victims of childbed fever. Although the role of micro-organisms in such infections had not yet been recognized at the time, Semmelweis realized that "cadaveric matter" which the student's scalpel had introduced into Kolletschka's blood stream had caused his colleague's fatal illness. And the similarities between the course of Kolletschka's disease and that of the women in his clinic led Semmelweis to the conclusion that his patients had died of the same kind of blood poisoning: he, his colleagues, and the medical students had been the carriers of the infectious material, for he and his associates used to come to the wards directly from performing dissections in the autopsy room, and examine the women in labor after only superficially washing their hands, which often retained a characteristic foul odor.

Again, Semmelweis put his idea to a test. He reasoned that if he were right, then childbed fever could be prevented by chemically destroying the infectious material adhering to the hands. He therefore issued an order requiring all medical students to wash their hands in a solution of chlorinated lime before making an examination. The mortality from childbed fever promptly began to decrease, and for the year 1848 it fell to 1.27 per cent in the First Division, compared to 1.33 in the Second.

In further support of his idea, or of his *hypothesis*, as we will also say, Semmelweis notes that it accounts for the fact that the mortality in the Second Division consistently was so much lower: the patients there were attended by midwives, whose training did not include anatomical instruction by dissection of cadavers.

The hypothesis also explained the lower mortality among "street births": women who arrived with babies in arms were rarely examined after admission and thus had a better chance of escaping infection.

Similarly, the hypothesis accounted for the fact that the victims of childbed fever among the newborn babies were all among those whose mothers had contracted the disease during labor; for then the infection could be transmitted to the baby before birth, through the common bloodstream of mother and child, whereas this was impossible when the mother remained healthy.

Further clinical experiences soon led Semmelweis to broaden his hypothesis. On one occasion, for example, he and his associates, having carefully disinfected their hands, examined first a woman in labor who was suffering from a festering cervical cancer; then they proceeded to examine twelve other women in the same room, after only routine washing without renewed disinfection. Eleven of the twelve patients died of puerperal fever. Semmelweis concluded that childbed fever can be caused not only by cadaveric material, but also by "putrid matter derived from living organisms."

2.2 Basic steps in testing a hypothesis

We have seen how, in his search for the cause of childbed fever, Semmelweis examined various hypotheses that had been suggested as possible answers. How such hypotheses are arrived at in the first place is an intriguing question which we will consider later. First, however, let us examine how a hypothesis, once proposed, is tested.

Sometimes, the procedure is quite direct. Consider the conjectures that differences in crowding, or in diet, or in general care account for the difference in mortality between the two divisions. As Semmelweis points out, these conflict with readily observable facts. There are no such differences between the divisions; the hypotheses are therefore rejected as false.

But usually the test will be less simple and straightforward. Take the hypothesis attributing the high mortality in the First Division to the dread evoked by the appearance of the priest with his attendant. The intensity of that dread, and especially its effect upon childbed fever, are not as directly ascertainable as are differences in crowding or in diet, and Semmelweis uses an indirect method of testing. He asks himself: Are there any readily observable effects that should occur if the hypothesis were true? And he reasons: If the hypothesis were true, *then* an appropriate change in the priest's procedure should be followed by a decline in fatalities. He checks this implication by a simple experiment and finds it false, and he therefore rejects the hypothesis.

Similarly, to test his conjecture about the position of the women during delivery, he reasons: If this conjecture should be true, *then* adoption of the lateral position in the First Division will reduce the mortality. Again, the implication is shown false by his experiment, and the conjecture is discarded.

In the last two cases, the test is based on an argument to the effect that *if* the contemplated hypothesis, say *H*, is true, *then* certain observable events (e.g., decline in mortality) should occur under specified circumstances (e.g., if the priest refrains from walking through the wards, or if the women are delivered in lateral position); or briefly, if *H* is true, then so is *I*, where *I* is a statement describing the observable occurrences to be expected. For convenience, let us say that *I* is inferred from, or implied by, *H*; and let us call *I* a *test implication of the hypothesis H*. (We will later give a more accurate description of the relation between *I* and *H*.)

In our last two examples, experiments show the test implication to be false, and the hypothesis is accordingly rejected. The reasoning that leads to the rejection may be schematized as follows:

If *H* is true, then so is *I*.
2*a*] But (as the evidence shows) *I* is not true.

H is not true.

Any argument of this form, called *modus tollens* in logic,[2] is deductively valid; that is, if its premises (the sentences above the horizontal line) are true, then its conclusion (the sentence below the horizontal line) is unfailingly true as well. Hence, if the premises of (2*a*) are properly established, the hypothesis *H* that is being tested must indeed be rejected.

Next, let us consider the case where observation or experiment bears out the test implication *I*. From his hypothesis that childbed fever is blood poisoning produced by cadaveric matter, Semmelweis infers that suitable antiseptic measures will reduce fatalities from the disease. This time, experiment shows the test implication to be true. But this favorable outcome does not conclusively prove the hypothesis true, for the underlying argument would have the form

If *H* is true, then so is *I*.
2*b*] (As the evidence shows) *I* is true.

H is true.

And this mode of reasoning, which is referred to as the *fallacy of affirming the consequent*, is deductively invalid, that is, its conclusion may be false even if its premises are true.[3] This is in fact illustrated by Semmelweis' own experience. The initial version of his account of childbed fever as a form of blood poisoning presented infection with cadaveric matter essentially as the one and only source of the disease; and he was right in reasoning that if this hypothesis should be true, then destruction

[2] For details, see another volume in this series: W. Salmon, *Logic*, pp. 24-25.
[3] See Salmon, *Logic*, pp. 27-29.

of cadaveric particles by antiseptic washing should reduce the mortality. Furthermore, his experiment did show the test implication to be true. Hence, in this case, the premisses of (*2b*) were both true. Yet, his hypothesis was false, for as he later discovered, putrid material from living organisms, too, could produce childbed fever.

Thus, the favorable outcome of a test, i.e., the fact that a test implication inferred from a hypothesis is found to be true, does not prove the hypothesis to be true. Even if many implications of a hypothesis have been borne out by careful tests, the hypothesis may still be false. The following argument still commits the fallacy of affirming the consequent:

If H is true, then so are $I_1, I_2, \ldots, I_n$.

2c]   (As the evidence shows) $I_1, I_2, \ldots, I_n$ are all true.

H is true.

This, too, can be illustrated by reference to Semmelweis' final hypothesis in its first version. As we noted earlier, his hypothesis also yields the test implications that among cases of street births admitted to the First Division, mortality from puerperal fever should be below the average for the Division, and that infants of mothers who escape the illness do not contract childbed fever; and these implications, too, were borne out by the evidence — even though the first version of the final hypothesis was false.

But the observation that a favorable outcome of however many tests does not afford conclusive proof for a hypothesis should not lead us to think that if we have subjected a hypothesis to a number of tests and all of them have had a favorable outcome, we are no better off than if we had not tested the hypothesis at all. For each of our tests might conceivably have had an unfavorable outcome and might have led to the rejection of the hypothesis. A set of favorable results obtained by testing different test implications, $I_1, I_2, \ldots, I_n$, of a hypothesis, shows that as far as these particular implications are concerned, the hypothesis has been borne out; and while this result does not afford a complete proof of the hypothesis, it provides at least some support, some partial corroboration or confirmation for it. The extent of this support will depend on various aspects of the hypothesis and of the test data. These will be examined in Chapter 4.

Let us now consider another example,[4] which will also bring to our attention some further aspects of scientific inquiry.

---

[4] The reader will find a fuller account of this example in Chap. 4 of J. B. Conant's fascinating book, *Science and Common Sense* (New Haven: Yale University Press, 1951). A letter by Torricelli setting forth his hypothesis and his test of it, and an eyewitness report on the Puy-de-Dôme experiment are reprinted in W. F. Magie, *A Source Book in Physics* (Cambridge: Harvard University Press, 1963), pp. 70-75.

As was known at Galileo's time, and probably much earlier, a simple suction pump, which draws water from a well by means of a piston that can be raised in the pump barrel, will lift water no higher than about 34 feet above the surface of the well. Galileo was intrigued by this limitation and suggested an explanation for it, which was, however, unsound. After Galileo's death, his pupil Torricelli advanced a new answer. He argued that the earth is surrounded by a sea of air, which, by reason of its weight exerts pressure upon the surface below, and that this pressure upon the surface of the well forces water up the pump barrel when the piston is raised. The maximum length of 34 feet for the water column in the barrel thus reflects simply the total pressure of the atmosphere upon the surface of the well.

It is evidently impossible to determine by direct inspection or observation whether this account is correct, and Torricelli tested it indirectly. He reasoned that *if* his conjecture were true, *then* the pressure of the atmosphere should also be capable of supporting a proportionately shorter column of mercury; indeed, since the specific gravity of mercury is about 14 times that of water, the length of the mercury column should be about 34/14 feet, or slightly less than 2½ feet. He checked this test implication by means of an ingeniously simple device, which was, in effect, the mercury barometer. The well of water is replaced by an open vessel containing mercury; the barrel of the suction pump is replaced by a glass tube sealed off at one end. The tube is completely filled with mercury and closed by placing the thumb tightly over the open end. It is then inverted, the open end is submerged in the mercury well, and the thumb is withdrawn; whereupon the mercury column in the tube drops until its length is about 30 inches—just as predicted by Torricelli's hypothesis.

A further test implication of that hypothesis was noted by Pascal, who reasoned that if the mercury in Torricelli's barometer is counterbalanced by the pressure of the air above the open mercury well, then its length should decrease with increasing altitude, since the weight of the air overhead becomes smaller. At Pascal's request, this implication was checked by his brother-in-law, Périer, who measured the length of the mercury column in the Torricelli barometer at the foot of the Puy-de-Dôme, a mountain some 4,800 feet high, and then carefully carried the apparatus to the top and repeated the measurement there while a control barometer was left at the bottom under the supervision of an assistant. Périer found the mercury column at the top of the mountain more than three inches shorter than at the bottom, whereas the length of the column in the control barometer had remained unchanged throughout the day.

We have considered some scientific investigations in which a problem was tackled by proposing tentative answers in the form of hypotheses that were then tested by deriving from them suitable test implications and checking these by observation or experiment.

But how are suitable hypotheses arrived at in the first place? It is sometimes held that they are inferred from antecedently collected data by means of a procedure called *inductive inference,* as contradistinguished from deductive inference, from which it differs in important respects.

In a deductively valid argument, the conclusion is related to the premisses in such a way that if the premisses are true then the conclusion cannot fail to be true as well. This requirement is satisfied, for example, by any argument of the following general form:

If p, then q.
It is not the case that q.

It is not the case that p.

Brief reflection shows that no matter what particular statements may stand at the places marked by the letters 'p' and 'q', the conclusion will certainly be true if the premisses are. In fact, our schema represents the argument form called *modus tollens,* to which we referred earlier.

Another type of deductively valid inference is illustrated by this example:

Any sodium salt, when put into the flame of a Bunsen burner, turns the flame yellow.
This piece of rock salt is a sodium salt.

This piece of rock salt, when put into the flame of a Bunsen burner, will turn the flame yellow.

Arguments of the latter kind are often said to lead from the general (here, the premiss about all sodium salts) to the particular (a conclusion about the particular piece of rock salt). Inductive inferences, by contrast, are sometimes described as leading from premisses about particular cases to a conclusion that has the character of a general law or principle. For example, from premisses to the effect that each of the particular samples of various sodium salts that have so far been subjected to the Bunsen flame test did turn the flame yellow, inductive inference supposedly leads to the general conclusion that all sodium salts, when put into the flame of a Bunsen burner, turn the flame yellow. But in this case, the truth of the premisses obviously does *not* guarantee the truth of the conclusion; for even if it is the case that all samples of sodium salts examined so far did turn the Bunsen flame yellow, it remains quite possible that new kinds of sodium salt might yet be found that do not conform to this generalization. Indeed, even some kinds of sodium salt that have already been tested with positive result might conceivably fail to satisfy the generalization under special physical conditions (such as very strong magnetic fields or the like) in which they have not yet been examined. For this reason, the premisses of an inductive inference are often said to imply the conclusion only with more or less high probability, whereas the premisses of a deductive inference imply the conclusion with certainty.

The idea that in scientific inquiry, inductive inference from antecedently collected data leads to appropriate general principles is clearly embodied in the following account of how a scientist would ideally proceed:

> If we try to imagine how a mind of superhuman power and reach, but normal so far as the logical processes of its thought are concerned, . . . would use the scientific method, the process would be as follows: First, all facts would be observed and recorded, *without selection* or *a priori* guess as to their relative importance. Secondly, the observed and recorded facts would be analyzed, compared, and classified, *without hypothesis or postulates* other than those necessarily involved in the logic of thought. Third, from this analysis of the facts generalizations would be inductively drawn as to the relations, classificatory or causal, between them. Fourth, further research would be deductive as well as inductive, employing inferences from previously established generalizations.[5]

This passage distinguishes four stages in an ideal scientific inquiry: (1) observation and recording of all facts, (2) analysis and classification of these facts, (3) inductive derivation of generalizations from them, and (4) further testing of the generalizations. The first two of these stages are specifically assumed not to make use of any guesses or hypotheses as to how the observed facts might be interconnected; this restriction seems to have been imposed in the belief that such preconceived ideas would introduce a bias and would jeopardize the scientific objectivity of the investigation.

But the view expressed in the quoted passage—I will call it *the narrow inductivist conception of scientific inquiry*—is untenable, for several reasons. A brief survey of these can serve to amplify and to supplement our earlier remarks on scientific procedure.

First, a scientific investigation as here envisaged could never get off the ground. Even its first phase could never be carried out, for a collection of *all* the facts would have to await the end of the world, so to speak; and even all the facts *up to now* cannot be collected, since there

[5] A. B. Wolfe, "Functional Economics," in *The Trend of Economics*, ed. R. G. Tugwell (New York: Alfred A. Knopf, Inc., 1924), p. 450 (italics are quoted).

are an infinite number and variety of them. Are we to examine, for example, all the grains of sand in all the deserts and on all the beaches, and are we to record their shapes, their weights, their chemical composition, their distances from each other, their constantly changing temperature, and their equally changing distance from the center of the moon? Are we to record the floating thoughts that cross our minds in the tedious process? The shapes of the clouds overhead, the changing color of the sky? The construction and the trade name of our writing equipment? Our own life histories and those of our fellow investigators? All these, and untold other things, are, after all, among "all the facts up to now".

Perhaps, then, all that should be required in the first phase is that all the *relevant* facts be collected. But relevant to what? Though the author does not mention this, let us suppose that the inquiry is concerned with a specified *problem*. Should we not then begin by collecting all the facts—or better, all available data—relevant to that problem? This notion still makes no clear sense. Semmelweis sought to solve one specific problem, yet he collected quite different kinds of data at different stages of his inquiry. And rightly so; for what particular sorts of data it is reasonable to collect is not determined by the problem under study, but by a tentative answer to it that the investigator entertains in the form of a conjecture or hypothesis. Given the conjecture that mortality from childbed fever was increased by the terrifying appearance of the priest and his attendant with the death bell, it was relevant to collect data on the consequences of having the priest change his routine; but it would have been totally irrelevant to check what would happen if doctors and students disinfected their hands before examining their patients. With respect to Semmelweis' eventual contamination hypothesis, data of the latter kind were clearly relevant, and those of the former kind totally irrelevant.

Empirical "facts" or findings, therefore, can be qualified as logically relevant or irrelevant only in reference to a given hypothesis, but not in reference to a given problem.

Suppose now that a hypothesis H has been advanced as a tentative answer to a research problem: what kinds of data would be relevant to H? Our earlier examples suggest an answer: A finding is relevant to H if either its occurrence or its nonoccurrence can be inferred from H. Take Torricelli's hypothesis, for example. As we saw, Pascal inferred from it that the mercury column in a barometer should grow shorter if the barometer were carried up a mountain. Therefore, any finding to the effect that this did indeed happen in a particular case is relevant to the hypotheses; but so would be the finding that the length of the mercury column had remained unchanged or that it had decreased and then increased during the ascent, for such findings would refute Pascal's test implication and would thus disconfirm Torricelli's hypothesis. Data of the former kind may be called positively, or favorably, relevant to the hypothesis; those of the latter kind negatively, or unfavorably, relevant.

In sum, the maxim that data should be gathered without guidance by antecedent hypotheses about the connections among the facts under study is self-defeating, and it is certainly not followed in scientific inquiry. On the contrary, tentative hypotheses are needed to give direction to a scientific investigation. Such hypotheses determine, among other things, what data should be collected at a given point in a scientific investigation.

It is of interest to note that social scientists trying to check a hypothesis by reference to the vast store of facts recorded by the U.S. Bureau of the Census, or by other data-gathering organizations, sometimes find to their disappointment that the values of some variable that plays a central role in the hypothesis have nowhere been systematically recorded. This remark is not, of course, intended as a criticism of data gathering: those engaged in the process no doubt try to select facts that might prove relevant to future hypotheses; the observation is simply meant to illustrate the impossibility of collecting "all the relevant data" without knowledge of the hypotheses to which the data are to have relevance.

The second stage envisaged in our quoted passage is open to similar criticism. A set of empirical "facts" can be analyzed and classified in many different ways, most of which will be unilluminating for the purposes of a given inquiry. Semmelweis could have classified the women in the maternity wards according to criteria such as age, place of residence, marital status, dietary habits, and so forth; but information on these would have provided no clue to a patient's prospects of becoming a victim of childbed fever. What Semmelweis sought were criteria that would be significantly connected with those prospects; and for this purpose, as he eventually found, it was illuminating to single out those women who were attended by medical personnel with contaminated hands; for it was with this characteristic, or with the corresponding class of patients, that high mortality from childbed fever was associated.

Thus, if a particular way of analyzing and classifying empirical findings is to lead to an explanation of the phenomena concerned, then it must be based on hypotheses about how those phenomena are connected; without such hypotheses, analysis and classification are blind.

Our critical reflections on the first two stages of inquiry as envisaged in the quoted passage also undercut the notion that hypotheses are introduced only in the third stage, by inductive inference from antecedently collected data. But some further remarks on the subject should be added here.

Induction is sometimes conceived as a method that leads, by means of mechanically applicable rules, from observed facts to corresponding general principles. In this case, the rules of inductive inference would provide effective canons of scientific discovery; induction would be a mechanical procedure analogous to the familiar routine for the multiplication of integers, which leads, in a finite number of predetermined and mechanically performable steps, to the corresponding product. Actually, however, no such general and mechanical induction procedure is available at present; otherwise, the much studied problem of the causation of cancer, for example, would hardly have remained unsolved to this day. Nor can the discovery of such a procedure ever be expected. For—to mention one reason—scientific hypotheses and theories are usually couched in terms that do not occur at all in the description of the empirical findings on which they rest, and which they serve to explain. For example, theories about the atomic and subatomic structure of matter contain terms such as 'atom', 'electron', 'proton', 'neutron', 'psi-function', etc.; yet they are based on laboratory findings about the spectra of various gases, tracks in cloud and bubble chambers, quantitative aspects of chemical reactions, and so forth—all of which can be described without the use of those "theoretical terms". Induction rules of the kind here envisaged would therefore have to provide a mechanical routine for constructing, on the basis of the given data, a hypothesis or theory stated in terms of some quite novel concepts, which are nowhere used in the description of the data themselves. Surely, no general mechanical rule of procedure can be expected to achieve this. Could there be a general rule, for example, which, when applied to the data available to Galileo concerning the limited effectiveness of suction pumps, would, by a mechanical routine, produce a hypothesis based on the concept of a sea of air?

To be sure, mechanical procedures for inductively "inferring" a hypothesis on the basis of given data may be specifiable for situations of special, and relatively simple, kinds. For example, if the length of a copper rod has been measured at several different temperatures, the resulting pairs of associated values for temperature and length may be represented by points in a plane coordinate system, and a curve may be drawn through them in accordance with some particular rule of curve fitting. The curve then graphically represents a general quantitative hypothesis that expresses the length of the rod as a specific function of its temperature. But note that this hypothesis contains no novel terms; it is expressible in terms of the concepts of temperature and length, which are used also in describing the data. Moreover, the choice of "associated" values of temperature and length as data already presupposes a guiding hypothesis; namely, that with each value of the temperature, exactly one value of the length of the copper rod is associated, so that its length is indeed a function of its temperature alone. The mechanical curve-fitting routine then serves only to select a particular function as the appropriate one. This point is important; for suppose that instead of a copper rod, we examine a body of nitrogen gas enclosed in a cylindrical container with a movable piston as a lid, and that we measure its volume at several different temperatures. If we were to use this procedure in an effort to obtain from our data a *general* hypothesis representing the volume of the gas as a function of its temperature, we would fail, because the volume of a gas is a function both of its temperature and of the pressure exerted upon it, so that at the same temperature, the given gas may assume different volumes.

Thus, even in these simple cases, the mechanical procedures for the construction of a hypothesis do only part of the job, for they presuppose an antecedent, less specific hypothesis (i.e., that a certain physical variable is a function of one single other variable), which is not obtainable by the same procedure.

There are, then, no generally applicable "rules of induction", by which hypotheses or theories can be mechanically derived or inferred from empirical data. The transition from data to theory requires creative imagination. Scientific hypotheses and theories are not *derived* from observed facts, but *invented* in order to account for them. They constitute guesses at the connections that might obtain between the phenomena under study, at uniformities and patterns that might underlie their occurrence. "Happy guesses" [6] of this kind require great ingenuity, especially if they involve a radical departure from current modes of scientific thinking, as did, for example, the theory of relativity and quantum theory. The inventive effort required in scientific research will benefit from a thorough familiarity with current knowledge in the field. A complete novice will hardly make an important scientific discovery, for the ideas that may occur to him are likely to duplicate what has been tried before or to run afoul of well-established facts or theories of which he is not aware.

Nevertheless, the ways in which fruitful scientific guesses are arrived at are very different from any process of systematic inference. The

---

[6] This characterization was given already by William Whewell in his work *The Philosophy of the Inductive Sciences*, 2nd ed. (London: John W. Parker, 1847); II, 41. Whewell also speaks of "invention" as "part of induction" (p. 46). In the same vein, K. Popper refers to scientific hypotheses and theories as "conjectures"; see, for example, the essay "Science: Conjectures and Refutations" in his book, *Conjectures and Refutations* (New York and London: Basic Books, 1962). Indeed, A. B. Wolfe, whose narrowly inductivist conception of ideal scientific procedure was quoted earlier, stresses that "the limited human mind" has to use "a greatly modified procedure", requiring scientific imagination and the selection of data on the basis of some "working hypothesis" (p. 450 of the essay cited in note 5).

chemist Kekulé, for example, tells us that he had long been trying un-successfully to devise a structural formula for the benzene molecule when, one evening in 1865, he found a solution to his problem while he was dozing in front of his fireplace. Gazing into the flames, he seemed to see atoms dancing in snakelike arrays. Suddenly, one of the snakes formed a ring by seizing hold of its own tail and then whirled mockingly before him. Kekulé awoke in a flash: he had hit upon the now famous and familiar idea of representing the molecular structure of benzene by a hexagonal ring. He spent the rest of the night working out the conse-quences of this hypothesis.[7]

This last remark contains an important reminder concerning the objectivity of science. In his endeavor to find a solution to his problem, the scientist may give free rein to his imagination, and the course of his creative thinking may be influenced even by scientifically questionable notions. Kepler's study of planetary motion, for example, was inspired by his interest in a mystical doctrine about numbers and a passion to demonstrate the music of the spheres. Yet, scientific objectivity is safe-guarded by the principle that while hypotheses and theories may be freely invented and *proposed* in science, they can be *accepted* into the body of scientific knowledge only if they pass critical scrutiny, which includes in particular the checking of suitable test implications by careful observation or experiment.

Interestingly, imagination and free invention play a similarly im-portant role in those disciplines whose results are validated exclusively by deductive reasoning; for example, in mathematics. For the rules of deductive inference do not afford mechanical rules of discovery, either. As illustrated by our statement of *modus tollens* above, those rules are usually expressed in the form of general schemata, any instance of which is a deductively valid argument. If premises of the specified kind are given, such a schema does indeed specify a way of proceeding to a logical consequence. But for any set of premises that may be given, the rules of deductive inference specify an infinity of validly deducible con-clusions. Take, for example, one simple rule represented by the following schema:

$$\frac{p}{p \text{ or } q}$$

It tells us, in effect, that from the proposition that p is the case, it follows that p or q is the case, where p and q may be any propositions whatever. The word 'or' is here understood in the "nonexclusive" sense, so that 'p

[7] Cf. the quotations from Kekulé's own report in A. Findlay, *A Hundred Years of Chemistry*, 2nd ed. (London: Gerald Duckworth & Co., 1948), p. 37; and W.I.B. Beveridge, *The Art of Scientific Investigation*, 3rd ed. (London: William Heine-mann, Ltd., 1957), p. 56.

or q' is tantamount to 'either p or q or both p and q'. Clearly, if the premiss of an argument of this type is true, then so must be the conclusion; hence, any argument of the specified form is valid. But this one rule alone entitles us to infer infinitely many different consequences from any one premiss. Thus, from 'the Moon has no atmosphere', it authorizes us to infer any statement of the form 'The Moon has no atmosphere, or q', where for 'q' we may write any statement whatsoever, no matter whether it is true or false; for example, 'the Moon's atmosphere is very thin', 'the Moon is uninhabited', 'gold is denser than silver', 'silver is denser than gold', and so forth. (It is interesting and not difficult to prove that infinitely many different statements can be formed in English; each of these may be put in the place of the variable 'q'.) Other rules of deductive inference add, of course, to the variety of statements derivable from one premiss or set of premisses. Hence, if we are given a set of statements as premisses, the rules of deduction give no direction to our inferential procedures. They do not single out one statement as "the" conclusion to be derived from our premisses, nor do they tell us how to obtain interesting or systematically important conclusions; they provide no mechanical routine, for example, for deriving significant mathematical theorems from given postulates. The discovery of important, fruitful mathematical theorems, like the discovery of important, fruitful theories in empirical science, requires inventive ingenuity; it calls for imaginative, insightful guessing. But again, the interests of scientific objectivity are safeguarded by the demand for an *objective validation* of such conjectures. In mathematics, this means *proof* by deductive derivation from axioms. And when a mathematical proposition has been proposed as a conjecture, its proof or disproof still requires inventiveness and ingenuity, often of a very high caliber; for the rules of deductive inference do not even provide a general mechanical procedure for constructing proofs or disproofs. Their systematic role is rather the modest one of serving as *criteria of soundness for arguments* offered as proofs: an argument will constitute a valid mathematical proof if it proceeds from the axioms to the proposed theorem by a chain of inferential steps each of which is valid according to one of the rules of deductive inference. And to check whether a given argument is a valid proof in this sense is indeed a purely mechanical task.

Scientific knowledge, as we have seen, is not arrived at by applying some inductive inference procedure to antecedently collected data, but rather by what is often called "the method of hypothesis", i.e. by inventing hypotheses as tentative answers to a problem under study, and then subjecting these to empirical test. It will be part of such test to see whether the hypothesis is borne out by whatever relevant findings may have been gathered before its formulation; an acceptable hypothesis will have to fit the available relevant data. Another part of the test will consist in deriving new test implications from the hypothesis and checking these by suitable observations or experiments. As we noted earlier, even extensive testing with entirely favorable results does not establish a hypothesis conclusively, but provides only more or less strong support for it. Hence, while scientific inquiry is certainly not inductive in the narrow sense we have examined in some detail, it may be said to be *inductive in a wider sense*, inasmuch as it involves the acceptance of hypotheses on the basis of data that afford no deductively conclusive evidence for it, but lend it only more or less strong "inductive support", or confirmation. And any "rules of induction" will have to be conceived, in analogy to the rules of deduction, as canons of validation rather than of discovery. Far from generating a hypothesis that accounts for given empirical findings, such rules will presuppose that both the empirical data forming the "premisses" of the "inductive argument" and a tentative hypothesis forming its "conclusion" are *given*. The rules of induction would then state criteria for the soundness of the argument. According to some theories of induction, the rules would determine the strength of the support that the data lend to the hypothesis, and they might express such support in terms of probabilities. In chapters 3 and 4 we will consider various factors that affect the inductive support and the acceptability of scientific hypotheses.

THE TEST OF A
HYPOTHESIS: ITS LOGIC
AND ITS FORCE

3

.1 Experimental
vs. nonexperi-
mental tests
Now we turn to a closer scrutiny of the reasoning on which scientific tests are based and of the conclusions that may be drawn from their outcomes. As before, we will use the word 'hypothesis' to refer to whatever statement is under test, no matter whether it purports to describe some particular fact or event or to express a general law or some other, more complex, proposition.

Let us begin with a simple remark, to which we will frequently have to refer in the subsequent discussion: the test implications of a hypothesis are normally of a conditional character; they tell us that *under specified test conditions*, an outcome of a certain kind will occur. Statements to this effect can be put into the following explicitly conditional form:

3a] If conditions of kind C are realized, then an event of kind E will occur.

For example, one of the hypotheses considered by Semmelweis yielded the test implication

If the patients in the First Division are delivered in lateral position, then their mortality from childbed fever will decrease.

And one of the test implications of his final hypothesis was

If the persons attending the women in the First Division wash their hands in a solution of chlorinated lime, then mortality from childbed fever will decrease.

Similarly, the test implications of Torricelli's hypothesis included conditional statements such as

If a Torricelli barometer is carried to increasing altitudes, then its mercury column will correspondingly decrease in length.

Such test implications are thus implications in a twofold sense: they are implications of the hypotheses from which they are derived, and they have the form of if then sentences, which in logic are called conditionals or material implications.

In each of the three examples just cited, the specified test conditions C are technologically realizable and can thus be brought about at will; and the realization of those conditions involves some control of a factor (position during delivery; absence or presence of infectious matter; pressure of the atmosphere overhead) that, according to the given hypothesis, affects the phenomenon under study (i.e., incidence of child-bed fever in the first two cases; length of the mercury column in the third). Test implications of this kind provide a basis for an *experimental test,* which amounts to bringing about the conditions C and checking whether E occurs as implied by the hypothesis.

Many scientific hypotheses are expressed in quantitative terms. In the simplest case, they will then represent the value of one quantitative variable as a mathematical function of certain other variables. Thus, the classical gas law, $V = c \cdot T/P$, represents the volume of a body of gas as a function of its temperature and pressure (c is a constant factor). A statement of this kind yields indefinitely many quantitative test implications. In our example, these are of the following form: if the temperature of a body of gas is T_1 and its pressure is P_1, then its volume is $c \cdot T_1/P_1$. And an experimental test then consists in varying the values of the "independent" variables and checking whether the "dependent" variable assumes the values implied by the hypothesis.

When experimental control is impossible, when the conditions C mentioned in the test implication cannot be brought about or varied by available technological means, then the hypothesis must be tested nonexperimentally, by seeking out, or waiting for, cases where the specified conditions are realized by nature, and then checking whether E does indeed occur.

It is sometimes said that in an experimental test of a quantitative hypothesis, only one of the quantities mentioned in the hypothesis is varied at a time, while all other conditions are kept constant. But this is impossible. In an experimental test of the gas law, for example, the pressure might be varied while the temperature is kept constant, or vice versa; but many other circumstances will change during the process—among them perhaps the relative humidity, the brightness of the illumination, and the strength of the magnetic field in the laboratory—and certainly the distance of the body of gas from the sun or moon. Nor is there any reason to try to keep as many as possible of these factors constant if the experiment is to test the gas law as specified. For the law states that the volume of a given body of gas is fully determined by its temperature and its pressure. It implies therefore that other factors are "irrelevant to the volume" in the sense that changes in these factors do not affect the volume of the gas. To allow such other factors to vary is therefore to explore a wider range of cases in search of possible violations of the hypothesis under test.

Experimentation, however, is used in science not only as a method of test, but also as a method of discovery; and in this second context, as we will now see, the requirement that certain factors be kept constant makes good sense.

The use of experimentation as a method of test is illustrated by Torricelli's and Périer's experiments. Here, a hypothesis has been antecedently advanced, and the experiment is performed to test it. In certain other cases, where no specific hypotheses have as yet been proposed, a scientist may start with a rough guess and may use experimentation as a guide to a more definite hypothesis. In studying how a metal wire is stretched by a weight suspended from it, he might conjecture that the quantitative increase in length will depend on the initial length of the wire, on its cross section, on the kind of metal it is made of, and on the weight of the body suspended from it. And he may then perform experiments to determine whether those factors do influence the increase in length (here, experimentation serves as a method of test), and if so, just how they affect the "dependent variable"—that is, just what the specific mathematical form of the dependence is (here, experimentation serves as a method of discovery). Knowing that the length of a wire varies also with its temperature, the experimenter will, first of all, keep the temperature constant, to eliminate the disturbing influence of this factor (though later on, he may systematically vary the temperature to ascertain whether the values of certain parameters in the functions connecting the length increase with the other factors are dependent on the temperature). In his experiments at constant temperature, he will vary the factors that he thinks are relevant, one at a time, keeping the others constant. On the basis of the results thus obtained, he will tentatively formulate generalizations that express the increase in length as a function of the unstretched length, of the weight, and so on; and from there, he may proceed to construct a more general formula representing the increase in length as a function of all the variables examined.

In cases of this kind, then, in which experimentation serves as a heuristic device, as a guide to the discovery of hypotheses, the principle of keeping all but one of the "relevant factors" constant makes good sense. But, of course, the most that can be done is to keep constant all but one of those factors that are believed to be "relevant" in the sense of affecting the phenomenon under study: it is always possible that some other important factors may have been overlooked.

It is one of the striking characteristics, and one of the great methodological advantages, of natural science that many of its hypotheses admit of experimental test. But experimental testing of hypotheses cannot be said to be a distinctive characteristic of all and only the natural sciences. It does not mark a dividing line between natural and social science, for experimental testing procedures are used also in psychology and, if to a lesser extent, in sociology. Also, the scope of experimental testing increases steadily with the advances in the requisite technology. Moreover, not all hypotheses in the natural sciences permit of experimental test. Take, for example, the law formulated by Leavitt and Shapley for the periodic fluctuations in the brightness of a certain type of variable star, the so-called classical Cepheids. The law states that the longer the period P of such a star, i.e., the time interval between two successive states of maximal brightness, the greater is its intrinsic luminosity; in quantitative terms, $M = -(a + b \cdot \log P)$, where M is the magnitude, which by definition varies inversely with the brightness of the star. This law deductively implies any number of test sentences stating what the magnitude of a Cepheid will be if its period has this or that particular value, for example, 5.3 days or 17.5 days. But Cepheids with specific periods cannot be produced at will; hence, the law cannot be tested by experiment. Rather, the astronomer must search the skies for new Cepheids and must then try to ascertain whether their magnitude and period conform to the presumptive law.

3.2 The role of auxiliary hypotheses   We said earlier that test implications are "derived" or "inferred" from the hypothesis that is to be tested. This statement, however, gives only a rough indication of the relationship between a hypothesis and the sentences that serve as its test implications. In some cases, it is indeed possible deductively to infer from a hypothesis certain conditional statements that can serve as test sentences for it. Thus, as we saw, the Leavitt-Shapley law deductively implies sentences of the form: 'If star s is a Cepheid with a period of so many days, then its magnitude will be such and such'. But often the "derivation" of a test implication is less simple and conclusive. Take, for example, Semmelweis' hypothesis that childbed fever is caused by contamination with infectious matter, and consider the test implication that if the persons attending the patients were to wash their hands in a solution of chlorinated lime, then mortality from childbed fever would be reduced. This statement does not follow deductively from the hypothesis alone; its derivation presupposes the further premiss that unlike soap and water alone, a chlorinated lime solution will destroy the infectious matter. This premiss, which is tacitly taken for granted in the argument, plays the role of what we will call an *auxiliary assumption,* or *auxiliary hypothesis,* in deriving the test sentence from Semmelweis' hypothesis. Hence, we are not entitled to assert here that if the hypothesis *H* is true then so must be the test implication *I*, but only that if both *H* and the auxiliary hypothesis are true then so will be *I*. Reliance on auxiliary hypotheses, as we shall see, is the rule rather than the exception in the testing of scientific hypotheses; and it has an important consequence for the question whether an unfavorable test finding, i.e., one that shows *I* to be false, can be held to disprove the hypothesis under investigation.

If *H* alone implies *I* and if empirical findings show *I* to be false, then *H* must also be qualified as false: this follows by the *modus tollens* argument (*2a*). But when *I* is derived from *H* in conjunction with one or more auxiliary hypotheses A, then the schema (*2a*) must be replaced by the following one:

> If both *H* and A are true, then so is *I*.
>
> *3b*] But (as the evidence shows) *I* is not true.
> _____
> *H* and A are not both true.

Thus if the test shows *I* to be false, we can infer only that either the hypothesis or one of the auxiliary assumptions included in A must be false; hence, the test provides no conclusive grounds for rejecting *H*. For example, if the antiseptic measure introduced by Semmelweis had not been followed by a decline in mortality, Semmelweis' hypothesis might still have been true: the negative test result might have been due to inefficacy of the chloride of lime solution as an antiseptic.

This kind of situation is not a mere abstract possibility. The astronomer Tycho Brahe, whose accurate observations provided the empirical basis for Kepler's laws of planetary motion, rejected the Copernican conception that the earth moves about the sun. He gave the following reason, among others: if the Copernican hypothesis were true, then the direction in which a fixed star would be seen by an observer on the earth at a fixed time of day should gradually change; for in the course of the annual travel of the earth about the sun, the star would be observed from a steadily changing vantage point—just as a child on a merry-go-round observes the face of an onlooker from a changing vantage point and therefore sees it in a constantly changing direction. More specifically, the direction from the observer to the star should vary periodically between two extremes, corresponding to opposite vantage points on the earth's orbit about the sun. The angle subtended by these points is called the annual parallax of the star; the farther the star is from the earth, the smaller will be its parallax. Brahe, who made his observations before the telescope was introduced, searched with his most precise instruments for evidence of such "parallactic motions" of fixed stars—and found none. He therefore rejected the hypothesis of the earth's motion. But the test implication that the fixed stars show observable parallactic motions can be derived from Copernicus' hypothesis only with the help of the auxiliary assumption that the fixed stars are so close to the earth that their parallactic movements are large enough to be detected by means of Brahe's instruments. Brahe was aware of making this auxiliary assumption, and he believed that he had grounds for regarding it as true; hence he felt obliged to reject the Copernican conception. It has since been found that the fixed stars do show parallactic displacements, but that Brahe's auxiliary hypothesis was mistaken: even the nearest fixed stars are vastly more remote than he had assumed, and therefore parallax measurements require powerful telescopes and very precise techniques. The first generally accepted measurement of a stellar parallax was made only in 1838.

The significance of auxiliary hypotheses in testing reaches still further. Suppose that a hypothesis H is tested by checking a test implication, 'If C then E', which has been derived from H and a set A of auxiliary hypotheses. The test then ultimately comes to checking whether or not E does occur in a test situation in which, to the best of the investigator's knowledge, the conditions C are realized. If in fact this is not the case—if, for example, the test equipment is faulty or not sufficiently sensitive—then E may fail to occur even if both H and A are true. For this reason, the total set of auxiliary assumptions presupposed by the test may be said to include the supposition that the test arrangement satisfies the specified conditions C.

This point is particularly important when the hypothesis under scrutiny has stood up well in previous tests and is an essential part of a larger system of interconnected hypotheses that is also supported by diverse other evidence. In such a case, an effort will likely be made to account for the nonoccurrence of E by showing that some of the conditions C were not satisfied in the test.

As an example, consider the hypothesis that electric charges have an atomistic structure and are all of them integral multiples of the charge of the atom of electricity, the electron. This hypothesis received very impressive support from experiments conducted by R. A. Millikan in 1909 and later. In these experiments, the electric charges on individual, extremely small drops of some liquid such as oil or mercury were determined by measuring the velocities of the droplets while they were falling in air under the influence of gravity or rising under the influence of a counteracting electric field. Millikan found all the charges either to be equal to, or to be small integral multiples of, a certain basic minimal charge, which he accordingly identified as the charge of the electron. On the basis of numerous careful measurements, he gave its value in electrostatic units as 4.774×10^{-10}. This hypothesis was soon challenged by the physicist Ehrenhaft in Vienna, who announced that he had repeated Millikan's experiment and had found charges that were considerably smaller than the electronic charge specified by Millikan. In his discussion of Ehrenhaft's results,[1] Millikan suggested several likely sources of error (i.e., violations of test requirements) that might account for Ehrenhaft's apparently adverse experimental findings: evaporation during observation, decreasing the weight of a droplet; formation of an oxide film on the mercury droplets used in some of Ehrenhaft's experiments; the disturbing influence of dust particles suspended in the air; the droplet drifting out of focus of the telescope used to observe it; deviation of very small droplets from the requisite spherical shape; inevitable errors in timing the movements of the small particles. In reference to two deviant particles observed and reported on by another investigator, who had experimented with oil drops, Millikan concludes: "The only possible interpretation then which could be put on these two particles . . . was that . . . they were not spheres of oil", but dust particles (pp. 170, 169). Millikan notes further that the results of more precise repetitions of his own experiment were all in essential accord with the result that he had announced earlier. Ehrenhaft continued for many years to defend and further expand his findings concerning subelectronic charges; but other physicists were not generally able to reproduce his results, and the atomistic conception of electric charge was maintained. Millikan's numerical value for the electronic charge, however, was later found to be slightly too small; interestingly, the deviation was traced to an error in one of Millikan's own auxiliary hypotheses: he had used too low a value for the viscosity of air in evaluating his oil drop data!

3.3 Crucial tests   The preceding remarks are of importance also for the idea of a crucial test, which can be briefly described as follows: suppose that H_1 and H_2 are two rival hypotheses concerning the same subject matter, which have so far stood up equally well in empirical tests, so that the available evidence does not favor one of them over the other. Then a decision between the two may be reached if some test can be specified for which H_1 and H_2 predict conflicting outcomes; i.e., if for a certain kind of test condition, C, the first hypothesis yields the test

[1] See Chap. VIII of R. A. Millikan, *The Electron* (Chicago: The University of Chicago Press, 1917). Reprinted, with an introduction by J.W.M. DuMond, 1963.

implication 'If C then E_1', and the second hypothesis yields 'If C then E_2', where E_1 and E_2 are mutually exclusive outcomes. Performance of the appropriate test will then presumably refute one of the hypotheses and support the other.

A classical example is the experiment performed by Foucault to decide between two competing conceptions of the nature of light. One of these, proposed by Huyghens and developed further by Fresnel and Young, held that light consists in transverse waves propagated in an elastic medium, the ether; the other was Newton's corpuscular conception, according to which light consists of extremely small particles traveling at high velocity. Either of these conceptions permitted the conclusion that light "rays" should conform to the laws of rectilinear propagation, reflection, and refraction. But the wave conception led to the further implication that light should travel faster in air than in water, whereas the corpuscular conception led to the opposite conclusion. In 1850, Foucault succeeded in performing an experiment in which the velocities of light in air and in water were directly compared. Images of two light-emitting points were produced by means of light rays that passed through water and through air, respectively, and were then reflected in a very rapidly revolving mirror. Depending on whether the velocity of light in air was greater or less than that in water, the image of the first light source would appear to the right or to the left of that of the second light source. The conflicting test implications checked by this experiment may therefore be briefly put as follows: 'if the Foucault experiment is performed, then the first image will appear to the right of the second image' and 'if the Foucault experiment is performed, then the first image will appear to the left of the second image'. The experiment showed the first of these implications to be true.

This outcome was widely regarded as a definitive refutation of the corpuscular conception of light and as a decisive vindication of the undulatory one. But this appraisal, though very natural, overrated the force of the test. For the statement that light travels faster in water than in air does not follow simply from the general conception of light rays as streams of particles; that assumption alone is much too indefinite to yield any specific quantitative consequences. Such implications as the laws of reflection and refraction and the statement about the velocities of light in air and in water can be derived only when the general corpuscular conception is supplemented by specific assumptions concerning the motion of the corpuscles and the influence exerted upon them by the surrounding medium. Newton did specify such assumptions; and in so doing, he set forth a definite *theory* [2] concerning the propagation of light. It is the total set of those basic theoretical principles that leads

---

[2] The form and function of theories will be further examined in Chap. 6.

to experimentally testable consequences such as the one checked by Foucault. Analogously, the wave conception was formulated as a *theory* based on a set of specific assumptions about the propagation of ether waves in different optical media; and again it is this set of theoretical principles that implied the laws of reflection and refraction and the statement that the velocity of light is greater in air than in water. Consequently—granting the truth of all other auxiliary hypotheses—the outcome of Foucault's experiment entitles us to infer only that not all the basic assumptions, or principles, of the corpuscular theory can be true—that at least one of them must be false. But it does not tell us which of them is to be rejected. Hence, it leaves open the possibility that the general conception of particle-like projectiles playing a role in the propagation of light might be retained in some modified form which would be characterized by a different set of basic laws.

And in fact, in 1905, Einstein did propound a modified version of the corpuscular conception in his theory of light quanta or photons, as they came to be called. The evidence he cited in support of his theory included an experiment performed by Lenard in 1903. Einstein characterized it as a "second crucial experiment" concerning the undulatory and corpuscular conceptions, and he noted that it "eliminated" the classical wave theory, in which by then the notion of elastic vibrations in the ether had been replaced by the idea, developed by Maxwell and Hertz, of transverse electromagnetic waves. Lenard's experiment, involving the photoelectric effect, could be regarded as testing two conflicting implications concerning the light energy that a radiating point P can transmit, during some fixed unit of time, to a small screen that is perpendicular to the light rays. On the classical wave theory, that energy will gradually and continuously decrease toward zero as the screen moves away from the point P; on the photon theory, the energy must be at least that carried by a single photon—unless during the given time interval, no photon strikes the screen, in which case the energy received will be zero; hence, there will be no continuous decrease to zero. Lenard's experiment had borne out this latter alternative. Again, however, the wave conception was not definitely refuted; the outcome of the experiment showed only that *some* modification was needed in the system of basic assumptions of the wave theory. Einstein, in fact, endeavored to modify the classical theory as little as possible.[3] In sum, then, an experiment of the kind here illustrated cannot strictly refute one of the two rival hypotheses.

But neither can it "prove" or definitively establish the other; for as was noted generally in section 2.2, scientific hypotheses or theories can-

[3] This example is discussed at some length in Chap. 8 of P. Frank, *Philosophy of Science* (Englewood Cliffs, N.J.: Prentice-Hall, Spectrum Books, 1962).

not be conclusively proved by any set of available data, no matter how accurate and extensive. This is particularly obvious for hypotheses or theories that assert or imply general laws either for some process that is not directly observable—as in the case of the rival theories of light— or for some phenomenon more readily accessible to observation and measurement, such as free fall. Galileo's law, for example, refers to *all* instances of free fall in the past, present, and future; whereas all the relevant evidence available at any time can cover only that relatively small set of cases—all of them belonging to the past—in which careful measurements have been carried out. And even if Galileo's law were found to be strictly satisfied in all the observed cases, this would obviously not preclude the possibility that some unobserved cases in past or future may not conform to it. In sum, even the most careful and extensive test can neither disprove one of two hypotheses nor prove the other: thus strictly construed, a crucial experiment is impossible in science.[4] But an experiment, such as Foucault's or Lenard's, may be crucial in a less strict, practical sense: it may reveal one of two conflicting theories as seriously inadequate and may lend strong support to its rival; and as a result, it may exert a decisive influence upon the direction of subsequent theorizing and experimentation.

3.4 Ad hoc hypotheses

If a particular way of testing a hypothesis *H presupposes* auxiliary assumptions $A_1, A_2, \ldots, A_n$—i.e., if these are used as additional premises in deriving from *H* the relevant test implication *I*—then, as we saw earlier, a negative test result, which shows *I* to be false, tells us only that *H* or one of the auxiliary hypotheses must be false and that a change must be made somewhere in this set of sentences if the test result is to be accommodated. A suitable adjustment might be made by modifying or completely abandoning *H* or by making changes in the system of auxiliary hypotheses. In principle, it would always be possible to retain *H* even in the face of seriously adverse test results—provided that we are willing to make sufficiently radical and perhaps burdensome revisions among our auxiliary hypotheses. But science is not interested in thus protecting its hypotheses or theories at all costs—and for good reasons. Consider an example. Before Torricelli introduced his conception of the pressure of the sea of air, the action of suction pumps was explained by the idea that nature abhors a vacuum and that, therefore, water rushes up the pump barrel to fill the vacuum created by the rising

---

[4] This is the famous verdict of the French physicist and historian of science, Pierre Duhem. Cf. Part II, Chap. VI of his book, *The Aim and Structure of Physical Theory*, trans. P. P. Wiener (Princeton: Princeton University Press, 1954), originally published in 1905. In his Foreword to the English translation, Louis de Broglie includes some interesting observations on this idea.

piston. The same idea also served to explain several other phenomena. When Pascal wrote to Périer asking him to perform the Puy-de-Dôme experiment, he argued that the expected outcome would be a "decisive" refutation of that conception: "If it happens that the height of the quicksilver is less at the top than at the base of the mountain . . . it follows of necessity that the weight and pressure of the air is the sole cause of this suspension of the quicksilver, and not the abhorrence of a vacuum: for it is quite certain that there is much more air that presses on the foot of the mountain than there is on its summit, and one cannot well say that nature abhors a vacuum more at the foot of the mountain than at its summit." [5] But the last remark actually indicates a way in which the conception of a *horror vacui* could be saved in the face of Périer's findings. Périer's results are decisive evidence against that conception only on the auxiliary assumption that the strength of the horror does not depend upon location. To reconcile Périer's apparently adverse evidence with the idea of a *horror vacui* it suffices to introduce instead the auxiliary hypothesis that nature's abhorrence of a vacuum decreases with increasing altitude. But while this assumption is not logically absurd or patently false, it is objectionable from the point of view of science. For it would be introduced *ad hoc*—i.e., for the sole purpose of saving a hypothesis seriously threatened by adverse evidence; it would not be called for by other findings and, roughly speaking, it leads to no additional test implications. The hypothesis of the pressure of air, on the other hand, does lead to further implications. Pascal mentions, for example, that if a partly inflated balloon were carried up a mountain, it would be more inflated at the mountaintop.

About the middle of the seventeenth century, a group of physicists, the plenists, held that a vacuum could not exist in nature; and in order to save this idea in the face of Torricelli's experiment, one of them offered the *ad hoc* hypothesis that the mercury in a barometer was being held in place by the "funiculus", an invisible thread by which it was suspended from the top of the inner surface of the glass tube. According to an initially very useful theory, developed early in the eighteenth century, the combustion of metals involves the escape of a substance called phlogiston. This conception was eventually abandoned in response to the experimental work of Lavoisier, who showed that the end product of the combustion process has greater weight than the original metal. But some tenacious adherents of the phlogiston theory tried to reconcile their conception with Lavoisier's finding by proposing the *ad hoc* hypoth-

[5] From Pascal's letter of November 15, 1647 in I.H.B. and A.G.H. Spiers, trans., *The Physical Treatises of Pascal* (New York: Columbia University Press, 1937), p. 101.

esis that phlogiston had negative weight, so that its escape would increase the weight of the residue.

We should remember, however, that with the benefit of hindsight, it seems easy to dismiss certain scientific suggestions of the past as *ad hoc* hypotheses, whereas it may be quite difficult to pass judgment on a hypothesis proposed in a contemporary context. There is, in fact, no precise criterion for *ad hoc* hypotheses, though the questions suggested earlier provide some guidance: is the hypothesis proposed just for the purpose of saving some current conception against adverse evidence, or does it also account for other phenomena, does it yield further significant test implications? And one further relevant consideration is this: if more and more qualifying hypotheses have to be introduced to reconcile a certain basic conception with new evidence that becomes available, the resulting total system will eventually become so complex that it has to give way when a simple alternative conception is proposed.

3.5 Testability-in-principle and empirical import

As the preceding discussion shows, no statement or set of statements T can be significantly proposed as a scientific hypothesis or theory unless it is amenable to objective empirical test, at least "in principle". This is to say that it must be possible to derive from T, in the broad sense we have considered, certain test implications of the form 'if test conditions C are realized, then outcome E will occur'; but the test conditions need not be realized or technologically realizable at the time when T is propounded or contemplated. Take the hypothesis, for example, that the distance covered in t seconds by a body falling freely from rest near the surface of the moon is $s = 2.7\, t^2$ feet. It yields deductively a set of test implications to the effect that the distances covered by such a body in 1, 2, 3, . . . seconds will be 2.7, 10.8, 24.3, . . . feet. Hence, the hypothesis is testable in principle, though it is as yet impossible to perform the test here specified.

But if a statement or set of statements is not testable at least in principle, in other words, if it has no test implications at all, then it cannot be significantly proposed or entertained as a scientific hypothesis or theory, for no conceivable empirical finding can then accord or conflict with it. In this case, it has no bearing whatever on empirical phenomena, or as we will also say, it lacks *empirical import*. Consider, for example, the view that the mutual gravitational attraction of physical bodies is a manifestation of certain "appetites or natural tendencies" closely related to love, inherent in those bodies, which make their "natural movements intelligible and possible".[6] What test implications can be derived from this interpretation of gravitational phenomena? Considering some char-

---

[6] This idea is set forth, for example, in J. F. O'Brien, "Gravity and Love as Unifying Principles," *The Thomist*, Vol. 21 (1958), 184-93.

acteristic aspects of love in the familiar sense, this view would seem to imply that gravitational affinity should be a selective phenomenon: not just any two physical bodies should attract each other. Nor should the strength of the affinity of one body to a second one always equal that of its converse, nor should it depend significantly on the masses of the bodies or on their distance. But since all of the consequences thus suggested are known to be false, the conception we are considering evidently is not meant to imply them. And indeed, that conception claims merely that the natural affinities underlying gravitational attraction are *related* to love. But, as will now be clear, this assertion is so elusive that it precludes the derivation of *any* test implications. No specific empirical findings of any kind are called for by this interpretation; no conceivable observational or experimental data can confirm or disconfirm it. In particular, therefore, it has no implications concerning gravitational phenomena; consequently, it cannot possibly explain those phenomena or render them "intelligible". To illustrate this further, let us suppose someone were to offer the alternative thesis that physical bodies gravitationally attract each other and tend to move toward each other from a natural tendency akin to hatred, from a natural inclination to collide with and destroy other physical objects. Would there be any conceivable way of adjudicating these conflicting views? Clearly not. Neither of them yields any testable implications; no empirical discrimination between them is possible. Not that the issue is "too deep" for scientific decision: the two verbally conflicting interpretations make no assertions at all. Hence, the question whether they are true or false makes no sense, and that is why scientific inquiry cannot possibly decide between them. They are *pseudo-hypotheses*: hypotheses in appearance only.

It should be borne in mind, however, that a scientific hypothesis normally yields test implications only when combined with suitable auxiliary assumptions. Thus, Torricelli's conception of the pressure exerted by the sea of air yields definite test implications only on the assumption that air pressure is subject to laws analogous to those for water pressure; this assumption underlies, for example, the Puy-de-Dôme experiment. In judging whether a proposed hypothesis does have empirical import, we should ask ourselves, therefore, what auxiliary hypotheses are explicitly or tacitly presupposed in the given context, and whether in conjunction with the latter, the given hypothesis yields test implications (other than those that may be derivable from the auxiliary assumptions alone).

Moreover, a scientific idea will often be introduced in an initial form that offers only limited and tenuous possibilities for test; and on the basis of such initial tests it will gradually be given a more definite, precise, and diversely testable form.

For these reasons, and for certain others which would lead us too far afield,[7] it is not possible to draw a sharp dividing line between hypotheses and theories that are testable in principle and those that are not. But even though it is somewhat vague, the distinction here referred to is important and illuminating for appraising the significance and the potential explanatory efficacy of proposed hypotheses and theories.

[7] The issue is discussed further in another volume of this series: William Alston, *Philosophy of Language*, Chap. 4. A fuller, technical discussion will be found in the essay, "Empiricist Criteria of Cognitive Significance: Problems and Changes," in C. G. Hempel, *Aspects of Scientific Explanation* (New York: The Free Press, 1965).

CRITERIA OF CONFIRMATION

AND ACCEPTABILITY

4

As we noted earlier, a favorable outcome of even very extensive and exacting tests cannot provide conclusive proof for a hypothesis, but only more or less strong evidential support, or confirmation. How strongly a hypothesis is supported by a given body of evidence depends on various characteristics of the evidence, which we will consider presently. In appraising what might be called the scientific acceptability or credibility of a hypothesis, one of the most important factors to consider is, of course, the extent and the character of the relevant evidence available and the resulting strength of the support it gives to the hypothesis. But several other factors have to be taken into account as well; these, too, will be surveyed in this chapter. We shall at first speak in a somewhat intuitive manner of more or less strong support, of small or large increments in confirmation, of factors that increase or decrease the credibility of a hypothesis, and the like. At the end of the chapter, we will briefly consider whether the concepts here referred to admit of a precise quantitative construal.

4.1 Quantity, variety, and precision of supporting evidence In the absence of unfavorable evidence, the confirmation of a hypothesis will normally be regarded as increasing with the number of favorable test findings. For example, each new Cepheid variable whose period and luminosity are found to conform to the Leavitt-Shapley law will be considered as adding to the evidential support of the law. But broadly speaking, the increase in confirmation effected by one new favorable instance will generally become smaller as the number of previously established favorable instances grows. If thousands of confirmatory cases are already available, the addition of one more favorable finding will raise the confirmation but little.

This remark must be qualified, however. If the earlier cases have all been obtained by tests of the same kind, but the new finding is the result of a different kind of test, the confirmation of the hypothesis may be significantly enhanced. For the confirmation of a hypothesis depends not only on the quantity of the favorable evidence available, but also on its variety: the greater the variety, the stronger the resulting support.

Suppose, for example, that the hypothesis under consideration is Snell's law, which states that a ray of light traveling obliquely from one optical medium into another is refracted at the separating surface in such a way that the ratio, $\sin \alpha / \sin \beta$, of the sines of the angles of incidence and of refraction is a constant for any pair of media. Compare now three sets of 100 tests each. In the first set, the media and the angle of incidence are kept constant: in each experiment, the ray passes from air into water at an angle of incidence of 30°; the angle of refraction is measured. Suppose that in all cases, $\sin \alpha / \sin \beta$ does have the same value. In the second set, the media are kept constant, but the angle α is varied: light passes from air into water at varying angles; β is measured. Again, suppose that $\sin \alpha / \sin \beta$ has the same value in all cases. In the third set, both the media and the angle α are varied: 25 different pairs of media are examined: for each pair, four different angles α are used. Suppose that for each pair of media, the four associated values of the ratio $\sin \alpha / \sin \beta$ are equal, while the ratios associated with different pairs have different values.

Each test set then presents a class of favorable outcomes, since the ratios associated with any particular pair of media are found to be equal, as implied by Snell's law. But the third set, which offers the greatest variety of positive instances, will surely be regarded as supporting the law much more strongly than the second, which provides supporting instances of much more limited variety; and the first set, it will be agreed, lends even less strong support to the general law. In fact, it might seem that in the first set, the same experiment is performed over and over again, and that the positive outcome in all 100 cases can support the hypothesis no more strongly than do the first two tests in the set, which bear out the constancy of the ratio. But this idea is mistaken. What is repeated here 100 times is not literally the same experiment, for the successive performances differ in many respects, such as the distance of the apparatus from the moon, perhaps the temperature of the light source, the atmospheric pressure, and so on. What is "kept the same" is simply a certain set of conditions, including a fixed angle of incidence and one particular pair of media. And even if the first two or more measurements under these circumstances yield the same value for sin α /sin β, it is logically quite possible that subsequent tests under the specified circumstances should yield different values for the ratio. Thus even here, repeated tests with favorable outcome add to the confirmation of the hypothesis—though much less so than do tests that cover a wider variety of instances.

We might recall here that Semmelweis was able to point to a considerable variety of facts that lent evidential support to his final hypothesis. Scientific theories are often supported by empirical findings of amazing variety. Newton's theory of gravitation and of motion implies, for example, the laws for free fall, for the simple pendulum, for the motion of the moon about the earth and of the planets about the sun, for the orbits of comets and of man-made satellites, for the motion of double stars about each other, for tidal phenomena, and many more. And all the diverse experimental and observational findings that bear out those laws lend support to Newton's theory.

The reason why diversity of evidence is so important a factor in the confirmation of a hypothesis might be suggested by the following consideration, which refers to our example of various tests for Snell's law. The hypothesis under test—let us call it S for short—refers to *all* pairs of optical media and asserts that for any pair, the ratio sin α /sin β has the same value for *all* associated angles of incidence and of refraction. Now, the more widely a set of experiments ranges over the diverse possibilities here covered, the greater will be the chances of finding an unfavorable instance if S should be false. Thus, the first set of experiments may be said to test more specifically a hypothesis S_1 that expresses only a small part of Snell's law—namely, that sin α /sin β has the same value whenever the optical media are air and water and α is 30°. Hence, if S_1 should be true, but S false, the first kind of test will never disclose this. Similarly, the second set of experiments tests a hypothesis S_2, which asserts distinctly more than S_1 but still not nearly as much as S—namely, that sin α /sin β has the same value for all angles α and the associated angles β if the media involved are air and water. Hence, if S_2 should be true, but S false, a test set of the second kind would never disclose this. Thus, the third set of experiments might be said to test Snell's law more thoroughly than the other two; an entirely favorable outcome accordingly lends stronger support to it.

As an additional illustration of the power of diversified evidence, we might note that if the diversity of the evidence is still further increased by varying the temperature of the optical media or by using monochromatic light of different wave lengths, then Snell's law in the classical form cited above is in fact found to be false.

But have we not overstated the case for diversified evidence? After all, some ways of increasing variety would be regarded as pointless, as incapable of raising the confirmation of a hypothesis. This verdict would apply, for example, if in our first test set for Snell's law the variety were increased by having the experiment performed at different places, during different phases of the moon, or by experimenters with different eye color. But to try such variations would not be unreasonable if as yet we had no knowledge, or only extremely limited knowledge, of what factors are likely to affect optical phenomena. At the time of the Puy-de-Dôme experiment, for example, the experimenters had no very definite ideas of what factors other than altitude might affect the length of the mercury column in the barometer; and when Pascal's brother-in-law and his associates performed the Torricelli experiment on the mountaintop and found the mercury column over three inches shorter than it had been at the foot of the mountain, they decided to repeat the experiment then and there, changing the circumstances in various ways. As Périer says in his report: "I therefore tried the same thing five times more, with great accuracy, at different places on the top of the mountain, once under cover in the little chapel which is there, once exposed, once in a shelter, once in the wind, once in good weather, and once during the rain and the mists which came over us sometimes, having taken care to get rid of the air in the tube every time; and in all these trials there was found the same height of the quicksilver . . . ; this result fully satisfied us." [1]

Thus, the qualification of certain ways of varying the evidence as important and of other ways as pointless is based on the background assumptions we entertain—perhaps as a result of previous research—concerning the probable influence of the factors to be varied upon the phenomenon with which the hypothesis is concerned.

And sometimes when such background assumptions are questioned and experimental variations are accordingly introduced which, on the generally accepted view, are pointless, a revolutionary discovery may be the outcome. This is illustrated by the recent overthrow of one of the basic background assumptions of physics, the principle of parity. According to this principle, the laws of nature are impartial between right and left; if a certain kind of physical process is possible (i.e., if its occurrence is not precluded by the laws of nature), then so is its mirror image (the process as seen in a reflecting mirror), where right and left are interchanged. In 1956, Yang and Lee, who were trying to account for some puzzling experimental findings concerning elementary particles, suggested that the principle of parity is violated in certain cases; and their bold hypothesis soon received clear experimental confirmation.

Sometimes, a test can be made more stringent, and its result the more weighty, by increasing the precision of the procedures of observa-

[1] W. F. Magie, ed., *A Source Book in Physics*, p. 74.

tion and measurement it involves. Thus, the hypothesis of the identity of inertial and gravitational mass—supported, for example, by the equality of the accelerations shown in free fall by bodies of different chemical constitution—has recently been re-examined with extremely precise methods; and the results, which have so far borne out the hypothesis, have greatly strengthened its confirmation.

2 Confirmation by "new" test implications

When a hypothesis is designed to explain certain observed phenomena, it will of course be so constructed that it implies their occurrence; hence, the fact to be explained will then constitute confirmatory evidence for it. But it is highly desirable for a scientific hypothesis to be confirmed also by "new" evidence—by facts that were not known or not taken into account when the hypothesis was formulated. Many hypotheses and theories in natural science have indeed received support from such "new" phenomena, with the result that their confirmation was considerably strengthened.

The point is well illustrated by an example that dates back to the last quarter of the nineteenth century, when physicists were searching for inherent regularities in the profusion of lines that had been found in the emission and absorption spectra of gases. In 1885, a Swiss school teacher, J. J. Balmer, proposed a formula that he thought expressed such a regularity for the wavelengths of a series of lines in the emission spectrum of hydrogen. On the basis of measurements that Ångström had made of four lines in that spectrum, Balmer constructed the following general formula:

$$\lambda = b \frac{n^2}{n^2 - 2^2}$$

Here, b is a constant, whose value Balmer determined empirically as 3645.6 Å, and n is an integer greater than 2. For n = 3, 4, 5, and 6, this formula yields values that agree very closely with those measured by Ångström; but Balmer was confident that the other values, too, would represent wavelengths of lines yet to be measured—or even yet to be found—in the hydrogen spectrum. He was unaware that some further lines had already been noted and measured. By now, 35 consecutive lines in the so-called Balmer series for hydrogen have been ascertained, and all of these have wavelengths that agree well with the values predicted by Balmer's formula.[2]

It is hardly surprising that such striking confirmation by correctly predicted "new" facts greatly enhances the credence we will be prepared

[2] A full and lucid account, on which this brief survey is based, will be found in Chap. 33 of G. Holton and D.H.D. Roller, *Foundations of Modern Physical Science* (Reading, Mass.: Addison-Wesley Publishing Co., 1958).

to give to a hypothesis. A puzzling question arises in this context. Suppose for a moment that Balmer's formula had been constructed only after all the 35 lines now recorded in the series had been carefully measured. In this fictitious case, then, exactly the same experimental findings would be available that have in fact been obtained by measurements made in part before, and in much larger part after, the constructions of the formula. Should that formula be considered as less well confirmed in the fictitious case than in the actual one? It might seem reasonable to answer in the affirmative, on these grounds: for *any* given set of quantitative data, it is possible to construct a hypothesis that covers them, just as for any finite set of points, it is possible to draw a smooth curve that contains them all. Thus, there would be nothing very surprising about the construction of Balmer's formula in our fictitious case. What *is* remarkable, and does lend weight to a hypothesis, is its fitting "new" cases: and Balmer's hypothesis has this accomplishment to its credit in the actual case, but not in the fictitious one. But this argument could be met with the reply that even in the fictitious case, Balmer's formula is not just some otherwise arbitrary hypothesis that is rigged to fit the 35 measured wavelengths: it is, rather, a hypothesis of striking formal simplicity; and the very fact that it subsumes those 35 wavelengths under a mathematically simple formula should lend it much higher credibility than could be accorded to a very complex formula fitting the same data. To state the idea in geometrical terms: if a set of points representing the results of measurements can be connected by a simple curve, we have much greater confidence in having discovered an underlying general law than if the curve is complicated and shows no perceptible regularity. (This notion of simplicity will be further considered, later on in this chapter.) Besides, from a logical point of view, the strength of the support that a hypothesis receives from a given body of data should depend only on what the hypothesis asserts and what the data are: the question of whether the hypothesis or the data were presented first, being a purely historical matter, should not count as affecting the confirmation of the hypothesis. This latter conception is certainly implicit in recently developed statistical theories of testing and also in some contemporary logical analyses of confirmation and induction, to which brief reference will be made at the end of this chapter.

4.3 Theoretical support   The support that may be claimed for a hypothesis need not all be of the inductive-evidential kind that we have considered so far: it need not consist entirely—or even partly—of data that bear out test implications derived from it. Support may also come "from above"; that is, from more inclusive hypotheses or theories that imply the given one and have independent evidential support. To illustrate: we considered earlier a hypothetical law for free fall on the moon, s = 2.7 t². Although none of its test implications have ever been checked by experiments on the moon, it has strong *theoretical support*, for it follows deductively from Newton's theory of gravitation and of motion (strongly supported by a highly diversified body of evidence) in conjunction with the information that the radius and the mass of the moon are .272 and .0123 of those of the earth and that the gravitational acceleration near the surface of the earth is 32.2 feet per second per second.

Similarly, the confirmation of a hypothesis that does have inductive-evidential support will be further strengthened if, in addition, it acquires deductive support from above. This happened, for example, to Balmer's formula. Balmer had anticipated the possibility that the hydrogen spectrum might contain further series of lines, and that the wavelengths of all the lines might conform to a generalization of his formula; namely,

$$\lambda = b \, \frac{n^2}{n^2 - m^2}$$

Here, m is a positive integer, and n is any integer greater than m. For $m = 2$, this generalization yields Balmer's formula; whereas $m = 1, 3, 4, \ldots$ determine new series of lines. And indeed, the existence of the series corresponding to $m = 1, 3, 4$, and 5 was later established by experimental exploration of the invisible infrared and ultraviolet parts of the hydrogen spectrum. Thus, there was strong evidential support for a more general hypothesis that implied Balmer's original formula as a special case, thus providing deductive support for it. And deductive support by a theory came in 1913, when the generalized formula—hence Balmer's original one, also—were shown by Bohr to be derivable from his theory of the hydrogen atom. This derivation greatly strengthened the support of Balmer's formula by fitting it into the context of quantum-theoretical conceptions developed by Planck, Einstein, and Bohr, which were supported by diverse evidence other than the spectroscopic measurements that lent inductive support to Balmer's formula.[3]

Correlatively, the credibility of a hypothesis will be adversely affected if it conflicts with hypotheses or theories that are accepted at the time as well-confirmed. In the *New York Medical Record* for 1877, a Dr. Caldwell of Iowa, reporting on an exhumation he claims to have witnessed, asserts that the hair and the beard of a man who had been buried clean-shaven, had burst the coffin and grown through the cracks.[4] Although presented by a presumptive eyewitness, this statement will be

---

[3] For details, see Holton and Roller, *Foundations of Modern Physical Science*, Chap. 34 (especially section 7).

[4] B. Evans, *The Natural History of Nonsense* (New York: Alfred A. Knopf, 1946), p. 133.

rejected without much hesitation because it conflicts with well-established findings about the extent to which human hair continues to grow after death.

Our earlier discussion of Ehrenhaft's claim to have experimentally established the existence of subelectronic charges similarly illustrates the point that conflict with a broadly supported theory militates against a hypothesis.

The principle here referred to must be applied with discretion and restraint, however. Otherwise, it could be used to protect any accepted theory against overthrow: adverse findings could always be dismissed as conflicting with a well-established theory. Science does not, of course, follow this procedure; it is not interested in defending certain pet conceptions against all possible adverse evidence. It aims, rather, at a comprehensive body of sound empirical knowledge, represented by a well-confirmed system of empirical statements, and it is accordingly prepared to give up or to modify whatever hypotheses it may have previously accepted. But findings that are to dislodge a well-established theory have to be weighty; and adverse experimental results, in particular, have to be repeatable. Even when a strong and useful theory has been found to conflict with an experimentally reproducible "effect", it may still continue to be used in contexts where it is not expected to lead into difficulties. For example, when Einstein propounded the theory of light quanta to account for such phenomena as the photoelectric effect, he noted that in dealing with the reflection, refraction, and polarization of light, the electromagnetic wave theory would probably never be replaced; and it is indeed still used in this context. A large-scale theory that has been successful in many areas will normally be abandoned only when a more satisfactory alternative theory is available—and good theories are difficult to come by.[5]

4.4 Simplicity   Another aspect that affects the acceptability of a hypothesis is its simplicity, compared with that of alternative hypotheses that would account for the same phenomena.

Consider a schematic illustration. Suppose that investigation of physical systems of a certain type (Cepheids, elastic metal springs, viscous liquids, or whatever) suggests to us that a certain quantitative characteristic, v, of such systems, might be a function of, and thus uniquely determined by, another such characteristic, u (in the way in

---

[5] This point is suggestively presented and illustrated by reference to the phlogiston theory of combustion in Chap. 7 of J. B. Conant, *Science and Common Sense*. A provocative general conception of the rise and fall of scientific theories is developed in T. S. Kuhn's book *The Structure of Scientific Revolutions* (Chicago: The University of Chicago Press, 1962).

which the period of a pendulum is a function of its length). We therefore try to construct a hypothesis stating the exact mathematical form
of the function. We have been able to check many instances in which u
had one of the values 0, 1, 2, or 3; the associated values of v were regu-
larly found to be 2, 3, 4, and 5, respectively. Suppose further that concerning these systems, we have no background knowledge that might
bear on the likely form of the functional connection, and that the following three hypotheses have been proposed on the basis of our data:

$$H_1: \quad v = u^4 - 6u^3 + 11u^2 - 5u + 2$$
$$H_2: \quad v = u^5 - 4u^4 - u^3 + 16u^2 - 11u + 2$$
$$H_3: \quad v = u + 2$$

Each of these fits the data: to each of the four u-values examined,
it assigns exactly the v-value that has been found associated with it.
In geometrical terms: if the three hypotheses are graphed in a plane
coordinate system, then each of the resulting curves contains the four
data-points (0,2), (1,3), (2,4), and (3,5).

Yet if, as has been assumed, we have no relevant background information that might indicate a different choice, we would no doubt
favor H_3 over H_1 and H_2 on the ground that it is a simpler hypothesis
than its rivals. This consideration suggests that if two hypotheses accord
with the same data and do not differ in other respects relevant to their
confirmation, the simpler one will count as more acceptable.

The relevance of the same basic idea to entire theories is often
illustrated by reference to the Copernican heliocentric conception of the
solar system, which was considerably simpler than the geocentric one it
came to supersede, namely, Ptolemy's ingenious and accurate, but "gor-
geously complicated system of main circles and sub-circles, with different
radii, speeds, tilts, and different amounts and directions of eccentricity."[6]

Though, undeniably, simplicity is highly prized in science, it is not
easy to state clear criteria of simplicity in the relevant sense and to justify
the preference given to simpler hypotheses and theories.

Any criteria of simplicity would have to be objective, of course; they
could not just refer to intuitive appeal or to the ease with which a
hypothesis or theory can be understood or remembered, etc., for these
factors vary from person to person. In the case of quantitative hypotheses
like H_1, H_2, H_3, one might think of judging simplicity by reference to
the corresponding graphs. In rectangular coordinates, the graph of H_3 is

[6] E. Rogers, *Physics for the Inquiring Mind* (Princeton: Princeton University
Press, 1960), p. 240. Chapters 14 and 16 of this work offer a splendid description
and appraisal of the two systems; they give more substance to the claim of greater
simplicity for Copernicus' scheme, but show also that it was able to account for
various facts, known at Copernicus' time, that the Ptolemaic system could not
explain.

a straight line, whereas graphs of H_1 and H_2 are much more complicated curves through the four data-points. But this criterion seems arbitrary. For if the hypotheses are represented in polar coordinates, with u as the direction angle and v as the radius vector, then H_3 determines a spiral, whereas a function determining a "simple" straight line would be quite complicated.

When, as in our example, all the functions are expressed by polynomials, the order of the polynomial might serve as an index of complexity; thus H_2 would be more complex than H_1, which in turn would be more complex than H_3. But further criteria are needed when trigonometric and other functions are to be considered as well.

In the case of theories, the number of independent *basic assumptions* is sometimes suggested as an indicator of complexity. But assumptions can be combined and split up in many ways: there is no unambiguous way of counting them. For example, the statement that for any two points there is exactly one straight line containing them might be counted as expressing two assumptions rather than one: that there is at least one such line, and that there is at most one. And even if we could agree on the count, different basic assumptions might in turn differ in complexity and would then have to be weighed rather than counted. Similar remarks apply to the suggestion that the number of *basic concepts* used in a theory might serve as an index of its complexity. The question of criteria of simplicity has in recent years received a good deal of attention from logicians and philosophers, and some interesting results have been obtained, but no satisfactory general characterization of simplicity is available. As our examples suggest, however, there certainly are cases in which, even in the absence of explicit criteria, investigators would be in substantial agreement about which of two competing hypotheses or theories is the simpler.

Another intriguing problem concerning simplicity is that of justification: what reasons are there for following the *principle of simplicity*, as we might call it; that is, the maxim that the simpler of two otherwise equally confirmed rival hypotheses or theories is to be preferred, is to count as more acceptable?

Many great scientists have expressed the conviction that the basic laws of nature are simple. If this were known, there would indeed be a presumption that the simpler of two rival hypotheses is more likely to be true. But the assumption that the basic laws of nature are simple is of course at least as problematic as the soundness of the principle of simplicity and thus cannot provide a justification for it.

Some scientists and philosophers—among them Mach, Avenarius, Ostwald, and Pearson—have held that science seeks to give an economic or parsimonious description of the world, and that general hypotheses purporting to express laws of nature are economic expedients for thought, serving to compress an indefinite number of particular cases (e.g., many cases of free fall) into one simple formula (e.g., Galileo's law); and from this point of view, it seems entirely reasonable to adopt the simplest among several competing hypotheses. This argument would be convincing if we had to choose between different *descriptions of one and the same set of facts*; but in adopting one among several competing hypotheses, such as H_1, H_2, H_3 above, we also adopt the *predictions* it implies concerning as yet untested cases; and in this respect, the hypotheses differ widely. Thus, for $u = 4$, H_1, H_2, and H_3 predict the v-values 150, 30, and 6, respectively. Now, H_3 may be mathematically simpler than its rivals; but what grounds are there for considering it more likely to be true, for basing our expectations concerning the as yet unexamined case $u = 4$ on H_3 rather than on one of the competing hypotheses, which fit the given data with the same precision?

One interesting answer has been suggested by Reichenbach.[7] Briefly, he argues as follows: suppose that in our example v is indeed a function of u, $v = f(u)$. Let g be its graph in some system of coordinates; the choice is inessential. The true function f and its graph are, of course, unknown to the scientist who measures associated values of the two variables. Assuming, for the sake of the argument, that his measurements are exact, he will thus find a number of data-points that lie on the "true" curve g. Suppose now that in accordance with the principle of simplicity, the scientist draws the simplest, i.e., the intuitively smoothest, curve through those points. Then his graph, say g_1, may deviate considerably from the true curve, though it does share at least the measured data-points with the latter. Put as the scientist determines more and more data-points and plots further simplest graphs, g_2, g_3, g_4, . . . , these will coincide more and more nearly with the true curve g, and the associated functions of f_2, f_3, f_4, . . . will approximate more and more closely the true functional connection f. Thus, observance of the principle of simplicity cannot be *guaranteed* to yield the function f in one step or even in many; but if there is a functional connection between u and v, the procedure will gradually lead to a function that approximates the true one to any desired degree.

Reichenbach's argument, which has here been stated in a somewhat simplified form, is ingenious; but its force is limited. For no matter how far the construction of successive graphs and functions may have gone, the procedure affords no indication at all of how close an approximation to the true function has been attained—if indeed there is a true function at all. (As we noted earlier, for example, the volume of a body

---

[7] H. Reichenbach, *Experience and Prediction* (Chicago: The University of Chicago Press, 1938), section 42.

of gas may seem to be, but is not in fact, a function of its temperature alone.) Moreover, the argument on grounds of convergence towards the true curve could be used also to justify certain other, intuitively complex and unreasonable methods of plotting graphs. For example, it is readily seen that if we were always to connect any two adjacent data-points by a semicircle whose diameter is the distance between the points, the resulting curves would eventually converge toward the true curve if there is one. Yet despite this "justification", this procedure would not be regarded as a sound way of forming quantitative hypotheses. Certain other nonsimple procedures, however—such as connecting adjacent data-points by hairpin loops whose length always exceeds a specified minimum value —are not justifiable in this fashion and can indeed be shown by Reichenbach's argument to be self-defeating. His idea is thus of distinct interest.

A very different view has been advanced by Popper. He construes the simpler of two hypotheses as the one that has greater empirical content, and he argues that the simpler hypothesis can therefore more readily be falsified (found out to be false), if indeed it should be false; and that this is of great importance to science, which seeks to expose its conjectures to the most thorough test and possible falsification. He summarizes his argument as follows: "Simple statements, if knowledge is our object, are to be prized more highly than less simple ones *because they tell us more; because their empirical content is greater; and because they are better testable.*"[8] Popper makes his notion of degree of simplicity as degree of falsifiability more explicit by means of two different criteria. According to one of them, the hypothesis that the orbit of a given planet is a circle is simpler than the hypothesis that it is an ellipse, because the former could be falsified by the determination of four positions that are found not to lie on a circle (three positions can always be connected by a circle), whereas the falsification of the second hypothesis would require the determination of at least six positions of the planet. In this sense, the simpler hypothesis is here the more readily falsifiable one, and it is also stronger because it logically implies the less simple hypothesis. This criterion surely contributes to clarifying the kind of simplicity that is of concern to science.

But Popper alternatively calls one hypothesis more falsifiable, and hence simpler, than another if the first implies the second and thus has greater content in a strictly deductive sense. However, greater content is surely not always linked to greater simplicity. To be sure, sometimes a strong theory, such as Newton's theory of gravitation and motion, will

---

[8] K. R. Popper, *The Logic of Scientific Discovery* (London: Hutchinson, 1959), p. 142 (italics are quoted). Chapters VI and VII of this book, which offer many illuminating observations on the role of simplicity in science, contain the presentation of the ideas here referred to.

be regarded as simpler than a vast array of unrelated laws of more limited scope that are implied by it. But the desirable kind of simplification thus achieved by a theory is not just a matter of increased content; for if two unrelated hypotheses (e.g., Hooke's and Snell's laws) are conjoined, the resulting conjunction tells us more, yet is not simpler, than either component. Also, of the three hypotheses H_1, H_2, H_3 considered above, none tells us more than any of the others; yet they do not count as equally simple. Nor do those three hypotheses differ in point of falsifiability. If false, any one of them can be shown to be false with the same ease—namely, by means of one counter-instance; for example, the data-pair (4, 10) would falsify them all.

Thus, while all the different ideas here briefly surveyed shed some light on the rationale of the principle of simplicity, the problems of finding a precise formulation and a unified justification for it are not as yet satisfactorily solved.[9]

4.5 The probability of hypotheses

Our survey of factors determining the credibility of scientific hypotheses shows that the credibility of a hypothesis H at a given time depends, strictly speaking, on the relevant parts of the total scientific knowledge at that time, including all the evidence relevant to the hypothesis and all the hypotheses and theories then accepted that have any bearing upon it; for as we have seen, it is by reference to these that the credibility of H has to be assessed. Strictly, therefore, we should speak of the *credibility of a hypothesis relative to a given body of knowledge*; the latter might be represented by a large set K of statements—all the statements accepted by science at the time.

The question naturally suggests itself whether it is possible to express this credibility in precise quantitative terms, by formulating a definition which, for any hypothesis H and any set K of statements, determines a number $c(H, K)$ expressing the degree of credibility that H possesses relative to K. And since we often speak of hypotheses as more or less probable, we might wonder further whether this quantitative concept could not be so defined as to satisfy all the basic principles of probability theory. In this case, the credibility of a hypothesis relative to any set K would be a real number no less than 0 and no greater than 1; a hypothesis that is true on purely logical grounds (such as 'Tomorrow it will rain in Central Park or it won't') would always have the credibility 1; and finally, for any two logically incompatible statements H_1 and H_2, the credibility of the hypothesis that one or the other of them is true

---

[9] The reader who wishes to pursue these issues further will find the following discussions helpful: S. Barker, *Induction and Hypothesis* (Ithaca: Cornell University Press, 1957); "A Panel Discussion of Simplicity of Scientific Theories," *Philosophy of Science*, Vol. 28 (1961), 109-71; W.V.O. Quine, "On Simple Theories of a Complex World," *Synthese*, Vol. 15 (1963), 103-6.

would equal the sum of their credibilities: $c(H_1 \text{ or } H_2, K) = c(H_1, K) + c(H_2, K)$.

Various theories for such probabilities have indeed been proposed.[10] They proceed from certain axioms like those just mentioned to a variety of more or less complex theorems that make it possible to determine certain probabilities *provided that others are already known*; but they offer no general definition of the probability of a hypothesis relative to given information.

And if the definition of the concept $c(H, K)$ is to take account of all the different factors we have surveyed, then the task is very difficult, to say the least; for as we saw, it is not even clear how such factors as the simplicity of a hypothesis, or the variety of its supporting evidence, are to be precisely characterized, let alone expressed in numerical terms.

However, certain illuminating and quite far-reaching results have recently been obtained by Carnap, who has studied the problem by reference to rigorously formalized model languages whose logical structure is considerably simpler than that required for the purpose of science. Carnap has developed a general method of defining what he calls the degree of confirmation for any hypothesis expressed in such a language with respect to any body of information expressed in the same language. The concept thus defined does satisfy all the principles of probability theory, and Carnap accordingly refers to it as the *logical* or *inductive probability* of the hypothesis relative to the given information.[11]

[10] One of them by the economist John Maynard Keynes, in his book, *A Treatise on Probability* (London: Macmillan & Company, Ltd., 1921).

[11] Carnap has given a brief and elementary account of the basic ideas in his article "Statistical and Inductive Probability," reprinted in E. H. Madden, ed., *The Structure of Scientific Thought* (Boston: Houghton Mifflin Company, 1960), pp. 269-79. A more recent, very illuminating statement is given in Carnap's article, "The Aim of Inductive Logic" in E. Nagel, P. Suppes, and A. Tarski, eds., *Logic, Methodology and Philosophy of Science*. Proceedings of the 1960 International Congress (Stanford: Stanford University Press, 1962), pp. 303-18.

LAWS AND THEIR ROLE

IN SCIENTIFIC EXPLANATION

5

To explain the phenomena of the physical world is one of the primary objectives of the natural sciences. Indeed, almost all of the scientific investigations that served as illustrations in the preceding chapters were aimed not at ascertaining some particular fact but at achieving some explanatory insight; they were concerned with questions such as how puerperal fever is contracted, why the water-lifting capacity of pumps has its characteristic limitation, why the transmission of light conforms to the laws of geometrical optics, and so forth. In this chapter and the next one, we will examine in some detail the character of scientific explanations and the kind of insight they afford.

That man has long and persistently been concerned to achieve some understanding of the enormously diverse, often perplexing, and sometimes threatening occurrences in the world around him is shown by the manifold myths and metaphors he has devised in an effort to account for the very existence of the world and of himself, for life and death, for the motions of the heavenly bodies, for the regular sequence of day and night, for the changing seasons, for thunder and lightning, sunshine and rain. Some of these explanatory ideas are based on anthropomorphic conceptions of the forces of nature, others invoke hidden powers or agents, still others refer to God's inscrutable plans or to fate.

Accounts of this kind undeniably may give the questioner a sense of having attained some understanding; they may resolve his perplexity and in this sense "answer" his question. But however satisfactory these answers may be psychologically, they are not adequate for the purposes of science, which, after all, is concerned to develop a conception of the world that has a clear, logical bearing on our experience and is thus capable of objective test. Scientific explanations must, for this reason, meet two systematic requirements, which will be called the requirement of explanatory relevance and the requirement of testability.

The astronomer Francesco Sizi offered the following argument to show why, contrary to what his contemporary, Galileo, claimed to have seen through his telescope, there could be no satellites circling around Jupiter:

> There are seven windows in the head, two nostrils, two ears, two eyes and a mouth; so in the heavens there are two favorable stars, two unpropitious, two luminaries, and Mercury alone undecided and indifferent. From which and many other similar phenomena of nature such as the seven metals, etc., which it were tedious to enumerate, we gather that the number of planets is necessarily seven. . . . Moreover, the satellites are invisible to the naked eye and therefore can have no influence on the earth and therefore would be useless and therefore do not exist.[1]

The crucial defect of this argument is evident: the "facts" it adduces, even if accepted without question, are entirely irrelevant to the point at issue; they do not afford the slightest reason for the assumption that Jupiter has no satellites; the claim of relevance suggested by the barrage of words like 'therefore', 'it follows', and 'necessarily' is entirely spurious.

Consider by contrast the physical explanation of a rainbow. It shows that the phenomenon comes about as a result of the reflection and refraction of the white light of the sun in spherical droplets of water such as those that occur in a cloud. By reference to the relevant optical laws, this account shows that the appearance of a rainbow is to be expected whenever a spray or mist of water droplets is illuminated by a strong white light behind the observer. Thus, even if we happened never to have seen a rainbow, the explanatory information provided by the physical account would constitute good grounds for expecting or believing that a rainbow will appear under the specified circumstances. We will refer to this characteristic by saying that the physical explanation meets the *requirement of explanatory relevance*: the explanatory information adduced affords good grounds for believing that the phenomenon to be explained did, or does, indeed occur. This condition must be met if we are to be entitled to say: "That explains it—the phenomenon in question was indeed to be expected under the circumstances!"

The requirement represents a necessary condition for an adequate explanation, but not a sufficient one. For example, a large body of data

---

[1] From Holton and Roller, *Foundations of Modern Physical Science*, p. 160.

showing a red-shift in the spectra of distant galaxies provides strong grounds for believing *that* those galaxies recede from our local one at enormous speeds, yet it does not explain *why*.

To introduce the second basic requirement for scientific explanations, let us consider once more the conception of gravitational attraction as manifesting a natural tendency akin to love. As we noted earlier, this conception has no test implications whatever. Hence, no empirical finding could possibly bear it out or disconfirm it. Being thus devoid of empirical content, the conception surely affords no grounds for expecting the characteristic phenomena of gravitational attraction: it lacks objective explanatory power. Similar comments apply to explanations in terms of an inscrutable fate: to invoke such an idea is not to achieve an especially profound insight, but to give up the attempt at explanation altogether. By contrast, the statements on which the physical explanation of a rainbow is based do have various test implications; these concern, for example, the conditions under which a rainbow will be seen in the sky, and the order of the colors in it; the appearance of rainbow phenomena in the spray of a wave breaking on the rocks and in the mist of a lawn sprinkler; and so forth. These examples illustrate a second condition for scientific explanations, which we will call the *requirement of testability*: the statements constituting a scientific explanation must be capable of empirical test.

It has already been suggested that since the conception of gravitation in terms of an underlying universal affinity has no test implications, it can have no explanatory power: it cannot provide grounds for expecting that universal gravitation will occur, nor that gravitational attraction will show such and such characteristic features; for if it did imply such consequences either deductively or even in a weaker, inductive-probabilistic sense, then it would be testable by reference to those consequences. As this example shows, the two requirements just considered are interrelated: a proposed explanation that meets the requirement of relevance also meets the requirement of testability. (The converse clearly does not hold.)

Now let us see what forms scientific explanations take, and how they meet the two basic requirements.

5.2 Deductive-nomological explanation

Consider once more Périer's finding in the Puy-de-Dôme experiment, that the length of the mercury column in a Torricelli barometer decreased with increasing altitude. Torricelli's and Pascal's ideas on atmospheric pressure provided an explanation for this phenomenon; somewhat pedantically, it can be spelled out as follows:

a]   At any location, the pressure that the mercury column in the closed branch of the Torricelli apparatus exerts upon the mercury below equals the pressure exerted on the surface of the mercury in the open vessel by the column of air above it.

b]   The pressures exerted by the columns of mercury and of air are proportional to their weights; and the shorter the columns, the smaller their weights.

c]   As Périer carried the apparatus to the top of the mountain, the column of air above the open vessel became steadily shorter.

d]   (Therefore,) the mercury column in the closed vessel grew steadily shorter during the ascent.

Thus formulated, the explanation is an argument to the effect that the phenomenon to be explained, as described by the sentence (*d*), is just what is to be expected in view of the explanatory facts cited in (*a*), (*b*), and (*c*); and that, indeed, (*d*) follows deductively from the explanatory statements. The latter are of two kinds; (*a*) and (*b*) have the character of general laws expressing uniform empirical connections; whereas (*c*) describes certain particular facts. Thus, the shortening of the mercury column is here explained by showing that it occurred in accordance with certain laws of nature, as a result of certain particular circumstances. The explanation fits the phenomenon to be explained into a pattern of uniformities and shows that its occurrence was to be expected, given the specified laws and the pertinent particular circumstances.

The phenomenon to be accounted for by an explanation will henceforth also be referred to as the *explanandum phenomenon*; the sentence describing it, as the *explanandum sentence*. When the context shows which is meant, either of them will simply be called the explanandum. The sentences specifying the explanatory information—(*a*), (*b*), (*c*) in our example—will be called the *explanans sentences*; jointly they will be said to form the *explanans*.

As a second example, consider the explanation of a characteristic of image formation by reflection in a spherical mirror; namely, that generally $1/u + 1/v = 2/r$, where u and v are the distances of object-point and image-point from the mirror, and r is the mirror's radius of curvature. In geometrical optics, this uniformity is explained with the help of the basic law of reflection in a plane mirror, by treating the reflection of a beam of light at any one point of a spherical mirror as a case of reflection in a plane tangential to the spherical surface. The resulting explanation can be formulated as a deductive argument whose conclusion is the explanandum sentence, and whose premises include the basic laws of reflection and of rectilinear propagation, as well as the statement that the surface of the mirror forms a segment of a sphere.[2]

A similar argument, whose premisses again include the law for reflection in a plane mirror, offers an explanation of why the light of a small light source placed at the focus of a paraboloidal mirror is reflected in a beam parallel to the axis of the paraboloid (a principle technologically applied in the construction of automobile headlights, searchlights, and other devices).

The explanations just considered may be conceived, then, as deductive arguments whose conclusion is the explanandum sentence, E, and whose premiss-set, the explanans, consists of general laws, L_1, L_2, ..., L_r and of other statements, C_1, C_2, ..., C_k, which make assertions about particular facts. The form of such arguments, which thus constitute one type of scientific explanation, can be represented by the following schema:

$$\text{D-N]} \quad \left. \begin{array}{c} L_1, L_2, \ldots, L_r \\[1em] C_1, C_2, \ldots, C_k \end{array} \right\} \text{Explanans sentences}$$

$$\overline{ E } \qquad \text{Explanandum sentence}$$

Explanatory accounts of this kind will be called explanations by deductive subsumption under general laws, or *deductive-nomological explanations*. (The root of the term 'nomological' is the Greek word 'nomos', for law.) The laws invoked in a scientific explanation will also be called *covering laws* for the explanandum phenomenon, and the explanatory argument will be said to subsume the explanandum under those laws.

The explanandum phenomenon in a deductive-nomological explanation may be an event occurring at a particular place and time, such as the outcome of Périer's experiment. Or it may be some regularity found in nature, such as certain characteristics generally displayed by rainbows; or a uniformity expressed by an empirical law such as Galileo's or Kepler's laws. Deductive explanations of such uniformities will then invoke laws of broader scope, such as the laws of reflection and refraction, or Newton's laws of motion and of gravitation. As this use of Newton's laws illustrates, empirical laws are often explained by means of theoretical principles that refer to structures and processes underlying the uniformities in question. We will return to such explanations in the next chapter.

---

[2] The derivation of the laws of reflection for the curved surfaces referred to in this example and in the next one is simply and lucidly set forth in Chap. 17 of Morris Kline, *Mathematics and the Physical World* (New York: Thomas Y. Crowell Company, 1959).

Deductive-nomological explanations satisfy the requirement of explanatory relevance in the strongest possible sense: the explanatory information they provide implies the explanandum sentence deductively and thus offers logically conclusive grounds why the explanandum phenomenon is to be expected. (We will soon encounter other scientific explanations, which fulfill the requirement only in a weaker, inductive, sense.) And the testability requirement is met as well, since the explanans implies among other things that under the specified conditions, the explanandum phenomenon occurs.

Some scientific explanations conform to the pattern (D-N) quite closely. This is so, particularly, when certain quantitative features of a phenomenon are explained by mathematical derivation from covering general laws, as in the case of reflection in spherical and paraboloidal mirrors. Or take the celebrated explanation, propounded by Leverrier (and independently by Adams), of peculiar irregularities in the motion of the planet Uranus, which on the current Newtonian theory could not be accounted for by the gravitational attraction of the other planets then known. Leverrier conjectured that they resulted from the gravitational pull of an as yet undetected outer planet, and he computed the position, mass, and other characteristics which that planet would have to possess to account in quantitative detail for the observed irregularities. His explanation was strikingly confirmed by the discovery, at the predicted location, of a new planet, Neptune, which had the quantitative characteristics attributed to it by Leverrier. Here again, the explanation has the character of a deductive argument whose premises include general laws —specifically, Newton's laws of gravitation and of motion—as well as statements specifying various quantitative particulars about the disturbing planet.

Not infrequently, however, deductive-nomological explanations are stated in an elliptical form: they omit mention of certain assumptions that are presupposed by the explanation but are simply taken for granted in the given context. Such explanations are sometimes expressed in the form 'E because C', where E is the event to be explained and C is some antecedent or concomitant event or state of affairs. Take, for example, the statement: 'The slush on the sidewalk remained liquid during the frost because it had been sprinkled with salt'. This explanation does not explicitly mention any laws, but it tacitly presupposes at least one: that the freezing point of water is lowered whenever salt is dissolved in it. Indeed, it is precisely by virtue of this law that the sprinkling of salt acquires the explanatory, and specifically causative, role that the elliptical because-statement ascribes to it. That statement, incidentally, is elliptical also in other respects; for example, it tacitly takes for granted, and leaves unmentioned, certain assumptions about the prevailing physical conditions, such as the temperature's not dropping to a very low point. And if nomic and other assumptions thus omitted are added to the statement that salt had been sprinkled on the slush, we obtain the premisses for a deductive-nomological explanation of the fact that the slush remained liquid.

Similar comments apply to Semmelweis's explanation that childbed fever was caused by decomposed animal matter introduced into the bloodstream through open wound surfaces. Thus formulated, the explanation makes no mention of general laws; but it presupposes that such contamination of the bloodstream generally leads to blood poisoning attended by the characteristic symptoms of childbed fever, for this is implied by the assertion that the contamination *causes* puerperal fever. The generalization was no doubt taken for granted by Semmelweis, to whom the cause of Kolletschka's fatal illness presented no etiological problem: given that infectious matter was introduced into the bloodstream, blood poisoning would result. (Kolletschka was by no means the first one to die of blood poisoning resulting from a cut with an infected scalpel. And by a tragic irony, Semmelweis himself was to suffer the same fate.) But once the tacit premiss is made explicit, the explanation is seen to involve reference to general laws.

As the preceding examples illustrate, corresponding general laws are always presupposed by an explanatory statement to the effect that a particular event of a certain kind G (e.g., expansion of a gas under constant pressure; flow of a current in a wire loop) was *caused* by an event of another kind, F (e.g., heating of the gas; motion of the loop across a magnetic field). To see this, we need not enter into the complex ramifications of the notion of cause; it suffices to note that the general maxim "Same cause, same effect", when applied to such explanatory statements, yields the implied claim that whenever an event of kind F occurs, it is accompanied by an event of kind G.

To say that an explanation rests on general laws is not to say that its discovery required the discovery of the laws. The crucial new insight achieved by an explanation will sometimes lie in the discovery of some particular fact (e.g., the presence of an undetected outer planet; infectious matter adhering to the hands of examining physicians) which, by virtue of antecedently accepted general laws, accounts for the explanandum phenomenon. In other cases, such as that of the lines in the hydrogen spectrum, the explanatory achievement does lie in the discovery of a covering law (Balmer's) and eventually of an explanatory theory (such as Bohr's); in yet other cases, the major accomplishment of an explanation may lie in showing that, and exactly how, the explanandum phenomenon can be accounted for by reference to laws and data about particular facts that are already available: this is illustrated by the explanatory derivation of the reflection laws for spherical and paraboloidal mirrors from the basic law of geometrical optics in conjunction with statements about the geometrical characteristics of the mirrors.

An explanatory problem does not by itself determine what kind of discovery is required for its solution. Thus, Leverrier discovered deviations from the theoretically expected course also in the motion of the planet Mercury; and as in the case of Uranus, he tried to explain these as resulting from the gravitational pull of an as yet undetected planet, Vulcan, which would have to be a very dense and very small object between the sun and Mercury. But no such planet was found, and a satisfactory explanation was provided only much later by the general theory of relativity, which accounted for the irregularities not by reference to some disturbing particular factor, but by means of a new system of laws.

5.3 Universal laws and accidental generalizations

As we have seen, laws play an essential role in deductive-nomological explanations. They provide the link by reason of which particular circumstances (described by C_1, C_2, . . . , C_k) can serve to explain the occurrence of a given event. And when the explanandum is not a particular event, but a uniformity such as those represented by characteristics mentioned earlier of spherical and paraboloidal mirrors, the explanatory laws exhibit a system of more comprehensive uniformities, of which the given one is but a special case.

The laws required for deductive-nomological explanations share a basic characteristic: they are, as we shall say, statements of universal form. Broadly speaking, a statement of this kind asserts a uniform connection between different empirical phenomena or between different aspects of an empirical phenomenon. It is a statement to the effect that whenever and wherever conditions of a specified kind F occur, then so will, always and without exception, certain conditions of another kind, G. (Not all scientific laws are of this type. In the sections that follow, we will encounter laws of probabilistic form, and explanations based on them.)

Here are some examples of statements of universal form: whenever the temperature of a gas increases while its pressure remains constant, its volume increases; whenever a solid is dissolved in a liquid, the boiling point of the liquid is raised; whenever a ray of light is reflected at a plane surface, the angle of reflection equals the angle of incidence; whenever a magnetic iron rod is broken in two, the pieces are magnets again; whenever a body falls freely from rest in a vacuum near the surface of the earth, the distance it covers in t seconds is $16t^2$ feet. Most of the laws of the natural sciences are quantitative: they assert specific mathematical connections between different quantitative characteristics of physical systems (e.g., between volume, temperature, and pressure of a gas) or of processes (e.g., between time and distance in free fall in Galileo's law; between the period of revolution of a planet and its mean distance from the sun, in Kepler's third law; between the angles of incidence and refraction in Snell's law).

Strictly speaking, a statement asserting some uniform connection will be considered a law only if there are reasons to assume it is true: we would not normally speak of false laws of nature. But if this requirement were rigidly observed, then the statements commonly referred to as Galileo's and Kepler's laws would not qualify as laws; for according to current physical knowledge, they hold only approximately; and as we shall see later, physical theory explains why this is so. Analogous remarks apply to the laws of geometrical optics. For example, even in a homogeneous medium, light does not move strictly in straight lines: it can bend around corners. We shall therefore use the word 'law' somewhat liberally, applying the term also to certain statements of the kind here referred to, which, on theoretical grounds, are known to hold only approximately and with certain qualifications. We shall return to this point when, in the next chapter, we consider the explanation of laws by theories.

We saw that the laws invoked in deductive-nomological explanations have the basic form: 'In all cases when conditions of kind F are realized, conditions of kind G are realized as well'. But, interestingly, not all statements of this universal form, even if true, can qualify as laws of nature. For example, the sentence 'All rocks in this box contain iron' is of universal form (F is the condition of being a rock in the box, G that of containing iron); yet even if true, it would not be regarded as a law, but as an assertion of something that "happens to be the case", as an "accidental generalization". Or consider the statement: 'All bodies consisting of pure gold have a mass of less than 100,000 kilograms'. No doubt all bodies of gold ever examined by man conform to it; thus, there is considerable confirmatory evidence for it and no disconfirming instances are known. Indeed, it is quite possible that never in the history of the universe has there been or will there be a body of pure gold with a mass of 100,000 kilograms or more. In this case, the proposed generalization would not only be well confirmed, but true. And yet, we would presumably regard its truth as accidental, on the ground that nothing in the basic laws of nature as conceived in contemporary science precludes the possibility of there being—or even the possibility of our producing—a solid gold object with a mass exceeding 100,000 kilograms.

Thus, a scientific law cannot be adequately defined as a true statement of universal form: this characterization expresses a necessary, but not a sufficient, condition for laws of the kind here under discussion.

What distinguishes genuine laws from accidental generalizations?

This intriguing problem has been intensively discussed in recent years. Let us look briefly at some of the principal ideas that have emerged from the debate, which is still continuing.

One telling and suggestive difference, noted by Nelson Goodman,[3] is this: a law can, whereas an accidental generalization cannot, serve to support *counterfactual conditionals*, i.e., statements of the form 'If A were (had been) the case, then B would be (would have been) the case', where in fact A is not (has not been) the case. Thus, the assertion 'If this paraffin candle had been put into a kettle of boiling water, it would have melted' could be supported by adducing the law that paraffin is liquid above 60 degrees centigrade (and the fact that the boiling point of water is 100 degrees centigrade). But the statement 'All rocks in this box contain iron' could not be used similarly to support the counterfactual statement 'If this pebble had been put into the box, it would contain iron'. Similarly, a law, in contrast to an accidentally true generalization, can support *subjunctive conditionals*, i.e., sentences of the type 'If A should come to pass, then so would B', where it is left open whether or not A will in fact come to pass. The statement 'If this paraffin candle should be put into boiling water then it would melt' is an example.

Closely related to this difference is another one, which is of special interest to us: a law can, whereas an accidental generalization cannot, serve as a basis for an explanation. Thus, the melting of a particular paraffin candle that was put into boiling water can be explained, in conformity with the schema (D-N), by reference to the particular facts just mentioned and to the law that paraffin melts when its temperature is raised above 60 degrees centigrade. But the fact that a particular rock in the box contains iron cannot be analogously explained by reference to the general statement that all rocks in the box contain iron.

It might seem plausible to say, by way of a further distinction, that the latter statement simply serves as a conveniently brief formulation of a finite conjunction of this kind: 'Rock r_1 contains iron, and rock r_2 contains iron, . . . , and rock r_{63} contains iron'; whereas the generalization about paraffin refers to a potentially infinite set of particular cases and therefore cannot be paraphrased by a finite conjunction of statements describing individual instances. This distinction is suggestive, but it is overstated. For to begin with, the generalization 'All rocks in this box contain iron' does not in fact tell us how many rocks there are in the box, nor does it name any particular rocks r_1, r_2, etc. Hence, the general

---

[3] In his essay, "The Problem of Counterfactual Conditionals," reprinted as the first chapter of his book, *Fact, Fiction, and Forecast*, 2nd ed. (Indianapolis: The Bobbs-Merrill Co., Inc., 1965). This work raises fascinating basic problems concerning laws, counterfactual statements, and inductive reasoning, and examines them from an advanced analytic point of view.

sentence is not logically equivalent to a finite conjunction of the kind just mentioned. To formulate a suitable conjunction, we need additional information, which might be obtained by counting and labeling the rocks in the box. Besides, our generalization 'All bodies of pure gold have a mass of less than 100,000 kilograms' would not count as a law even if there were infinitely many bodies of gold in the world. Thus, the criterion we have under consideration fails on several grounds.

Finally, let us note that a statement of universal form may qualify as a law even if it actually has no instances whatever. As an example, consider the sentence: 'On any celestial body that has the same radius as the earth but twice its mass, free fall from rest conforms to the formula $s = 32\ t^2$ '. There might well be no celestial object in the entire universe that has the specified size and mass, and yet the statement has the character of a law. For it (or rather, a close approximation of it, as in the case of Galileo's law) follows from the Newtonian theory of gravitation and of motion in conjunction with the statement that the acceleration of free fall on the earth is 32 feet per second per second; thus, it has strong theoretical support, just like our earlier law for free fall on the moon.

A law, we noted, can support subjunctive and counterfactual conditional statements about potential instances, i.e., about particular cases that might occur, or that might have occurred but did not. In similar fashion, Newton's theory supports our general statement in a subjunctive version that suggests its lawlike status, namely: 'On any celestial body that there may be which has the same size as the earth but twice its mass, free fall would conform to the formula $s = 32t^2$ '. By contrast, the generalization about the rocks cannot be paraphrased as asserting that any rock that might be in this box would contain iron, nor of course would this latter claim have any theoretical support.

Similarly, we would not use our generalization about the mass of gold bodies—let us call it H—to support statements such as this: 'Two bodies of pure gold whose individual masses add up to more than 100,000 kilograms cannot be fused to form one body; or if fusion should be possible, then the mass of the resulting body will be less than 100,000 kg', for the basic physical and chemical theories of matter that are currently accepted do not preclude the kind of fusion here considered, and they do not imply that there would be a mass loss of the sort here referred to. Hence, even if the generalization H should be true, i.e., if no exceptions to it should ever occur, this would constitute a mere accident or coincidence as judged by current theory, which permits the occurrence of exceptions to H.

Thus, whether a statement of universal form counts as a law will depend in part upon the scientific theories accepted at the time. This is not to say that "empirical generalizations"—statements of universal form that are empirically well confirmed but have no basis in theory— never qualify as laws: Galileo's, Kepler's, and Boyle's laws, for example, were accepted as such before they received theoretical grounding. The relevance of theory is rather this: a statement of universal form, whether empirically confirmed or as yet untested, will qualify as a law if it is implied by an accepted theory (statements of this kind are often referred to as theoretical laws); but even if it is empirically well confirmed and presumably true in fact, it will not qualify as a law if it rules out certain hypothetical occurrences (such as the fusion of two gold bodies with a resulting mass of more than 100,000 kilograms, in the case of our generalization H) which an accepted theory qualifies as possible.[4]

5.4 Probabilistic explanation: fundamentals

Not all scientific explanations are based on laws of strictly universal form. Thus, little Jim's getting the measles might be explained by saying that he caught the disease from his brother, who had a bad case of the measles some days earlier. This account again links the explanandum event to an earlier occurrence, Jim's exposure to the measles; the latter is said to provide an explanation because there is a connection between exposure to the measles and contracting the disease. That connection cannot be expressed by a law of universal form, however; for not every case of exposure to the measles produces contagion. What can be claimed is only that persons exposed to the measles will contract the disease with high probability, i.e., in a high percentage of all cases. General statements of this type, which we shall soon examine more closely, will be called *laws of probabilistic form* or *probabilistic laws*, for short.

In our illustration, then, the explanans consists of the probabilistic law just mentioned and the statement that Jim was exposed to the measles. In contrast to the case of deductive-nomological explanation, these explanans statements do not deductively imply the explanandum statement that Jim got the measles; for in deductive inferences from true premises, the conclusion is invariably true, whereas in our example, it is clearly possible that the explanans statements might be true and yet the explanandum statement false. We will say, for short, that the explanans implies the explanandum, not with "deductive certainty", but only with near-certainty or with high probability.

The resulting explanatory argument may be schematized as follows at the top of page 59.

---

[4] For a fuller analysis of the concept of law, and for further bibliographic references, see E. Nagel, *The Structure of Science* (New York: Harcourt, Brace & World, Inc., 1961), Chap. 4.

The probability for persons exposed to the measles
to catch the disease is high.

Jim was exposed to the measles.

————————————————————— [makes highly probable]

Jim caught the measles.

In the customary presentation of a deductive argument, which was used, for example, in the schema (D-N) above, the conclusion is separated from the premises by a single line, which serves to indicate that the premises logically imply the conclusion. The double line used in our latest schema is meant to indicate analogously that the "premises" (the explanans) make the "conclusion" (the explanandum sentence) more or less probable; the degree of probability is suggested by the notation in brackets.

Arguments of this kind will be called *probabilistic explanations*. As our discussion shows, a probabilistic explanation of a particular event shares certain basic characteristics with the corresponding deductive-nomological type of explanation. In both cases, the given event is explained by reference to others, with which the explanandum event is connected by laws. But in one case, the laws are of universal form; in the other, of probabilistic form. And while a deductive explanation shows that, on the information contained in the explanans, the explanandum was to be expected with "deductive certainty", an inductive explanation shows only that, on the information contained in the explanans, the explanandum was to be expected with high probability, and perhaps with "practical certainty"; it is in this manner that the latter argument meets the requirement of explanatory relevance.

5.5 Statistical probabilities and probabilistic laws

We must now consider more closely the two differentiating features of probabilistic explanation that have just been noted: the probabilistic laws they invoke and the peculiar kind of probabilistic implication that connects the explanans with the explanandum.

Suppose that from an urn containing many balls of the same size and mass, but not necessarily of the same color, successive drawings are made. At each drawing, one ball is removed, and its color is noted. Then the ball is returned to the urn, whose contents are thoroughly mixed before the next drawing takes place. This is an example of a so-called random process or random experiment, a concept that will soon be characterized in more detail. Let us refer to the procedure just described as experiment U, to each drawing as one performance of U, and to the color of the ball produced by a given drawing as the result, or the outcome, of that performance.

If all the balls in an urn are white, then a statement of strictly universal form holds true of the results produced by the performance of

U: every drawing from the urn yields a white ball, or yields the result W, for short. If only some of the balls—say, 600 of them—are white, whereas the others—say 400—are red, then a general statement of probabilistic form holds true of the experiment: the probability for a performance of U to produce a white ball, or outcome W, is .6; in symbols:

5a] $P(W,U) = .6$

Similarly, the probability of obtaining heads as a result of the random experiment C of flipping a fair coin is given by

5b] $P(H,C) = .5$

and the probability of obtaining an ace as a result of the random experiment D of rolling a regular die is

5c] $P(A,D) = 1/6$

What do such probability statements mean? According to one familiar view, sometimes called the "classical" conception of probability, the statement (5a) would have to be interpreted as follows: each performance of the experiment U effects a choice of one from among 1,000 basic possibilities, or basic alternatives, each represented by one of the balls in the urn; of these possible choices, 600 are "favorable" to the outcome W; and the probability of drawing a white ball is simply the ratio of the number of favorable choices available to the number of all possible choices, i.e., 600/1,000. The classical interpretation of the probability statements (5b) and (5c) follows similar lines.

Yet this characterization is inadequate; for if before each drawing, the 400 red balls in the urn were placed on top of the white ones, then in this new kind of urn experiment—let us call it U'—the ratio of favorable to possible basic alternatives would remain the same, but the probability of drawing a white ball would be smaller than in the experiment U, in which the balls are thoroughly mixed before each drawing. The classical conception takes account of this difficulty by requiring that the basic alternatives referred to in its definition of probability must be "equipossible" or "equiprobable"—a requirement presumably violated in the case of experiment U'.

This added proviso raises the question of how to define equipossibility or equiprobability. We will pass over this notoriously troublesome and controversial issue, because—even assuming that equiprobability can be satisfactorily characterized—the classical conception would still be inadequate, since probabilities are assigned also to the outcomes of random experiments for which no plausible way is known of marking off equiprobable basic alternatives. Thus, for the random experiment D of rolling a regular die, the six faces might be regarded as representing such equiprobable alternatives; but we attribute probabilities to such results as rolling an ace, or an odd number of points, etc., also in the case of a loaded die, even though no equiprobable basic outcomes can be marked off here.

Similarly—and this is particularly important—science assigns probabilities to the outcomes of certain random experiments or random processes encountered in nature, such as the step-by-step decay of the atoms of radioactive substances, or the transition of atoms from one energy state to another. Here again, we find no equiprobable basic alternatives in terms of which such probabilities might be classically defined and computed.

To arrive at a more satisfactory construal of our probability statements, let us consider how one would ascertain the probability of the rolling of an ace with a given die that is not known to be regular. This would obviously be done by making a large number of throws with the die and ascertaining the *relative frequency*, i.e., the proportion, of those cases in which an ace turns up. If, for example, the experiment D' of rolling the given die is performed 300 times and an ace turns up in 62 cases, then the relative frequency, 62/300, would be regarded as an approximate value of the probability $p(A,D')$ of rolling an ace with the given die. Analogous procedures would be used to estimate the probabilities associated with the flipping of a given coin, the spinning of a roulette wheel, and so on. Similarly, the probabilities associated with radioactive decay, with the transitions between different atomic energy states, with genetic processes, etc., are determined by ascertaining the corresponding relative frequencies; however, this is often done in highly indirect ways rather than by simply counting individual atomic or other events of the relevant kinds.

The interpretation in terms of relative frequencies applies also to probability statements such as (5b) and (5c), which concern the results of flipping a fair (i.e., homogeneous and strictly cylindrical) coin or tossing a regular (homogeneous and strictly cubical) die: what the scientist (or the gambler, for that matter) is concerned with in making a probability statement is the relative frequency with which a certain outcome O can be expected in long series of repetitions of some random experiment R. The counting of "equiprobable" basic alternatives and of those among them which are "favorable" to O may be regarded as a heuristic device for guessing at the relative frequency of O. And indeed when a regular die or a fair coin is tossed a large number of times, the different faces tend to come up with equal frequency. One might expect this on the basis of symmetry considerations of the kind frequently used in forming physical hypotheses, for our empirical knowledge affords no grounds on which to expect any of the faces to be favored over any other. But while such considerations often are heuristically useful, they must not be regarded as certain or as self-evident truths: some very plausible symmetry assumptions, such as the principle of parity, have been found not to be generally satisfied at the subatomic level. Assumptions about equiprobabilities are therefore always subject to correction in the light of empirical data concerning the actual relative frequencies of the phenomena in question. This point is illustrated also by the statistical theories of gases developed by Bose and Einstein and by Fermi and Dirac, respectively, which rest on different assumptions concerning what distributions of particles over a phase space are equiprobable.

The probabilities specified in the probabilistic laws, then, represent relative frequencies. They cannot, however, be strictly defined as relative frequencies in long series of repetitions of the relevant random experiment. For the proportion, say, of aces obtained in throwing a given die will change, if perhaps only slightly, as the series of throws is extended; and even in two series of exactly the same length, the number of aces will usually differ. We do find, however, that as the number of throws increases, the relative frequency of each of the different outcomes tends to change less and less, even though the results of successive throws continue to vary in an irregular and practically unpredictable fashion. This is what generally characterizes a random experiment R with outcomes $O_1, O_2, ... O_n$: successive performances of R yield one or another of those outcomes in an irregular manner; but the relative frequencies of the outcomes tend to become stable as the number of performances increases. And the probabilities of the outcomes, $p(O_1,R)$, $p(O_2,R),...,p(O_n,R)$, may be regarded as ideal values that the actual frequencies tend to assume as they become increasingly stable. For mathematical convenience, the probabilities are sometimes defined as the mathematical *limits* toward which the relative frequencies converge as the number of performances increases indefinitely. But this definition has certain conceptual shortcomings, and in some more recent mathematical studies of the subject, the intended empirical meaning of the concept of probability is deliberately, and for good reasons, characterized more vaguely by means of the following so-called *statistical interpretation of probability:* [5]

The statement

$$p(O,R) = r$$

means that in a long series of performances of random experiment R,

[5] Further details on the concept of statistical probability and on the limit-definition and its shortcomings will be found in E. Nagel's monograph, *Principles of the Theory of Probability* (Chicago: University of Chicago Press, 1939). Our version of the statistical interpretation follows that given by H. Cramér on pp. 148-49 of his book, *Mathematical Methods of Statistics* (Princeton: Princeton University Press, 1946).

the proportion of cases with outcome O is almost certain to be close to r.

The concept of *statistical probability* thus characterized must be carefully distinguished from the concept of *inductive or logical probability*, which we considered in section 4.5. Logical probability is a quantitative logical relation between definite *statements*; the sentence

$$c(H,K) = r$$

asserts that the hypothesis H is supported, or made probable, to degree r by the evidence formulated in statement K. Statistical probability is a quantitative relation between repeatable *kinds of events:* a certain kind of outcome, O, and a certain kind of random process, R; it represents, roughly speaking, the relative frequency with which the result O tends to occur in a long series of performances of R.

What the two concepts have in common are their mathematical characteristics: both satisfy the basic principles of mathematical probability theory:

a] The possible numerical values of both probabilities range from 0 to 1:

$$0 \leq p(O,R) \leq 1$$
$$0 \leq c(H,K) \leq 1$$

b] The probability for one of two mutually exclusive outcomes of R to occur is the sum of the probabilities of the outcomes taken separately; the probability, on any evidence K, for one or the other of two mutually exclusive hypotheses to hold is the sum of their respective probabilities:

If 0_1, 0_2 are mutually exclusive, then
$$p(0_1 \text{ or } 0_2, R) = p(0_1,R) + p(0_2,R)$$
If H_1, H_2 are logically exclusive hypotheses, then
$$c(H_1 \text{ or } H_2, K) = c(H_1,K) + c(H_2,K)$$

c] The probability of an outcome that necessarily occurs in all cases—such as O or not O—is 1; the probability, on any evidence, of a hypothesis that is logically (and in this sense necessarily) true, such as H or not H, is 1:

$$p(0 \text{ or not } 0, R) = 1$$
$$c(H \text{ or not } H, K) = 1$$

Scientific hypotheses in the form of statistical probability statements can be, and are, tested by examining the long-run relative frequencies of the outcomes concerned; and the confirmation of such hypotheses is then judged, broadly speaking, in terms of the closeness of the agreement between hypothetical probabilities and observed frequencies. The logic of such tests, however, presents some intriguing special problems, which call for at least brief examination.

Consider the hypothesis, H, that the probability of rolling an ace with a certain die is .15; or briefly, that $p(A,D) = .15$, where D is the random experiment of rolling the given die. The hypothesis H does not deductively imply any test implications specifying how many aces will occur in a finite series of throws of the die. It does not imply, for example, that exactly 75 among the first 500 throws will yield an ace, nor even that the number of aces will lie between 50 and 100, say. Hence, if the proportion of aces actually obtained in a large number of throws differs considerably from .15, this does not refute H in the sense in which a hypothesis of strictly universal form, such as 'All swans are white', can be refuted, in virtue of the *modus tollens* argument, by reference to one counter-instance, such as a black swan. Similarly, if a long run of throws of the given die yields a proportion of aces very close to .15, this does not confirm H in the sense in which a hypothesis is confirmed by the finding that a test sentence I that it logically implies is in fact true. For in this latter case, the hypothesis asserts I by logical implication, and the test result is thus confirmatory in the sense of showing that a certain part of what the hypothesis asserts is indeed true; but nothing strictly analogous is shown for H by confirmatory frequency data; for H does *not* assert by implication that the frequency of aces in some long run will definitely be very close to .15.

But while H does not logically preclude the possibility that the proportion of aces obtained in a long series of throws of the given die may depart widely from .15, it does logically imply that such departures are highly improbable in the statistical sense; i.e., that if the experiment of performing a long series of throws (say, 1,000 of them per series) is repeated a large number of times, then only a tiny proportion of those long series will yield a proportion of aces that differs considerably from .15. For the case of rolling a die, it is usually assumed that the results of successive throws are "statistically independent"; this means roughly that the probability of obtaining an ace in a throw of the die does not depend on the result of the preceding throw. Mathematical analysis shows that in conjunction with this independence assumption, our hypothesis H deductively determines the statistical probability for the proportion of aces obtained in n throws to differ from .15 by no more than a specified amount. For example, H implies that for a series of 1,000 throws of the die here considered, the probability is about .976 that the proportion of aces will lie between .125 and .175; and similarly, that for a run of 10,000 throws the probability is about .995 that the proportion of aces will be between .14 and .16. Thus, we may say that if H is true, then it is practically certain that in a long trial run the observed proportion of aces will differ by very little from the hypothetical probability value .15. Hence, if the observed long-run frequency of an outcome is not close to the probability assigned to it by a given probabilistic hypothesis, then that hypothesis is very likely to be false. In this case, the frequency data count as disconfirming the hypothesis, or as reducing its credibility; and if sufficiently strong disconfirming evidence is found, the hypothesis will be considered as practically, though not logically, refuted and will accordingly be rejected. Similarly, close agreement between hypothetical probabilities and observed frequencies will tend to confirm a probabilistic hypothesis and may lead to its acceptance.

If probabilistic hypotheses are to be accepted or rejected on the basis of statistical evidence concerning observed frequencies, then appropriate standards are called for. These will have to determine (a) what deviations of observed frequencies from the probability stated by a hypothesis are to count as grounds for rejecting the hypothesis, and (b) how close an agreement between observed frequencies and hypothetical probability is to be required as a condition for accepting the hypothesis. The requirements in question can be made more or less strict, and their specification is a matter of choice. The stringency of the chosen standards will normally vary with the context and the objectives of the research in question. Broadly speaking, it will depend on the importance that is attached, in the given context, to avoiding two kinds of error that might be made: rejecting the hypothesis under test although it is true, and accepting it although it is false. The importance of this point is particularly clear when acceptance or rejection of the hypothesis is to serve as a basis for practical action. Thus, if the hypothesis concerns the probable effectiveness and safety of a new vaccine, then the decision about its acceptance will have to take into account not only how well the statistical test results accord with the probabilities specified by the hypothesis, but also how serious would be the consequences of accepting the hypothesis and acting on it (e.g. by inoculating children with the vaccine) when in fact it is false, and of rejecting the hypothesis and acting accordingly (e.g. by destroying the vaccine and modifying or discontinuing the process of manufacture) when in fact the hypothesis is true. The complex problems that arise in this context form the subject matter of the theory of statistical tests and decisions, which has been developed in recent decades on the basis of the mathematical theory of probability and statistics.[6]

Many important laws and theoretical principles in the natural sciences are of probabilistic character, though they are often of more

---

[6] On this subject, see R. D. Luce and H. Raiffa, *Games and Decisions* (New York: John Wiley & Sons, Inc., 1957).

complicated form than the simple probability statements we have discussed. For example, according to current physical theory, radioactive decay is a random phenomenon in which the atoms of each radioactive element possess a characteristic probability of disintegrating during a specified period of time. The corresponding probabilistic laws are usually formulated as statements giving the "half-life" of the element concerned. Thus, the statements that the half-life of radium^{226} is 1,620 years and that of polonium^{218} is 3.05 minutes are laws to the effect that the probability for a radium^{226} atom to decay within 1,620 years, and for an atom of polonium^{218} to decay within 3.05 minutes, are both one-half. According to the statistical interpretation cited earlier, these laws imply that of a large number of radium^{226} atoms or of polonium^{218} atoms given at a certain time, very close to one-half will still exist 1,620 years, or 3.05 minutes, later; the others having disintegrated by radioactive decay.

Again, in the kinetic theory various uniformities in the behavior of gases, including the laws of classical thermodynamics, are explained by means of certain assumptions about the constituent molecules; and some of these are probabilistic hypotheses concerning statistical regularities in the motions and collisions of those molecules.

A few additional remarks concerning the notion of a probabilistic law are indicated. It might seem that all scientific laws should be qualified as probabilistic since the supporting evidence we have for them is always a finite and logically inconclusive body of findings, which can confer upon them only a more or less high probability. But this argument misses the point that the distinction between laws of universal form and laws of probabilistic form does not refer to the strength of the evidential support for the two kinds of statements, but to their form, which reflects the logical character of the claim they make. A law of universal form is basically a statement to the effect that in *all* cases where conditions of kind *F* are realized, conditions of kind *G* are realized as well; a law of probabilistic form asserts, basically, that under certain conditions, constituting the performance of a random experiment *R*, a certain kind of outcome will occur in a specified percentage of cases. No matter whether true or false, well supported or poorly supported, these two types of claims are of a logically different character, and it is on this difference that our distinction is based.

As we saw earlier, a law of the universal form 'Whenever *F* then *G*' is by no means a brief, telescoped equivalent of a report stating for each occurrence of *F* so far examined that it was associated with an occurrence of *G*. Rather, it implies assertions also for all unexamined cases of *F*, past as well as present and future; also, it implies counterfactual and hypothetical conditionals which concern, so to speak "possible occurrences" of *F*: and it is just this characteristic that gives such laws their explanatory power. Laws of probabilistic form have an analogous status. The law stating that the radioactive decay of radium^{226} is a random process with an associated half-life of 1,620 years is plainly not tantamount to a report about decay rates that have been observed in certain samples of radium^{226}. It concerns the decaying process of any body of radium^{226}—past, present, or future; and it implies subjunctive and counterfactual conditionals, such as: if two particular lumps of radium^{226} were to be combined into one, the decay rates would remain the same as if the lumps had remained separate. Again, it is this characteristic that gives probabilistic laws their predictive and their explanatory force.

5.6 The inductive character of probabilistic explanation

One of the simplest kinds of probabilistic explanation is illustrated by our earlier example of Jim's catching the measles. The general form of that explanatory argument may be stated thus:

$$\frac{\begin{array}{l} p(0,R) \text{ is close to } 1 \\ i \text{ is a case of R} \end{array}}{i \text{ is a case of } 0} \quad \text{[makes highly probable]}$$

Now the high probability which, as indicated in brackets, the explanans confers upon the explanandum is surely not a statistical probability, for it characterizes a relation between sentences, not between (kinds of) events. Using a term introduced in Chapter 4, we might say that the probability in question represents the rational credibility of the explanandum, given the information provided by the explanans; and as we noted earlier, in so far as this notion can be construed as a probability, it represents a logical or inductive probability.

In some simple cases, there is a natural and obvious way of expressing that probability in numerical terms. In an argument of the kind just considered, if the numerical value of $p(O,R)$ is specified, then it is reasonable to say that the inductive probability that the explanans confers upon the explanandum has the same numerical value. The resulting probabilistic explanation has the form:

$$\frac{\begin{array}{l} p(0,R) = r \\ i \text{ is a case of R} \end{array}}{i \text{ is a case of } 0} \quad \text{[r]}$$

If the explanans is more complex, the determination of corresponding inductive probabilities for the explanandum raises difficult problems, which in part are still unsettled. But whether or not it is possible to assign definite numerical probabilities to all such explanations, the preceding considerations show that when an event is explained by reference to probabilistic laws, the explanans confers upon the explanandum only more or less strong inductive support. Thus, we may distinguish deductive-nomological from probabilistic explanations by saying that the former effect a deductive subsumption under laws of universal form, the latter an inductive subsumption under laws of probabilistic form.

It is sometimes said that precisely because of its inductive character, a probabilistic account does not explain the occurrence of an event, since the explanans does not logically preclude its nonoccurrence. But the important, steadily expanding role that probabilistic laws and theories play in science and its applications, makes it preferable to view accounts based on such principles as affording explanations as well, though of a less stringent kind than those of deductive-nomological form. Take, for example, the radioactive decay of a sample of one milligram of polonium²¹⁸. Suppose that what is left of this initial amount after 3.05 minutes is found to have a mass that falls within the interval from .499 to .501 milligrams. This finding can be explained by the probabilistic law of decay for polonium²¹⁸; for that law, in combination with the principles of mathematical probability, deductively implies that given the huge number of atoms in a milligram of polonium²¹⁸, the probability of the specified outcome is overwhelmingly large, so that in a particular case its occurrence may be expected with "practical certainty".

Or consider the explanation offered by the kinetic theory of gases for an empirically established generalization called Graham's law of diffusion. The law states that at fixed temperature and pressure, the rates at which different gases in a container escape, or diffuse, through a thin porous wall are inversely proportional to the square roots of their molecular weights; so that the amount of a gas that diffuses through the wall per second will be the greater, the lighter its molecules. The explanation rests on the consideration that the mass of a given gas that diffuses through the wall per second will be proportional to the average velocity of its molecules, and that Graham's law will therefore have been explained if it can be shown that the average molecular velocities of different pure gases are inversely proportional to the square roots of their molecular weights. To show this, the theory makes certain assumptions broadly to the effect that a gas consists of a very large number of molecules moving in random fashion at different speeds that frequently change as a result of collisions, and that this random behavior shows certain probabilistic uniformities—in particular, that among the molecules of a given gas at specified temperature and pressure, different velocities will occur with definite, and different, probabilities. These assumptions make it possible to compute the probabilistically expected values—or, as we might briefly say, the "most probable" values—that the average velocities of different gases will possess at equal temperatures and pressures. These most probable average values, the theory shows, are indeed inversely proportional to the square roots of the molecular weights of the gases. But the actual diffusion rates, which are measured experimentally and are the subject of Graham's law, will depend on the actual values that the average velocities have in the large but finite swarms of molecules constituting the given bodies of gas. And the actual average values are related to the corresponding probabilistically estimated, or "most probable", values in a manner that is basically analogous to the relation between the proportion of aces occurring in a large but finite series of tossings of a given die and the corresponding probability of rolling an ace with that die. From the theoretically derived conclusion concerning the probabilistic estimates, it follows only that in view of the very large number of molecules involved, it is overwhelmingly *probable* that at any given time the actual average speeds will have values very close to their probability estimates and that, therefore, it is *practically certain* that they will be, like the latter, inversely proportional to the square roots of their molecular masses, thus satisfying Graham's law.[7]

It seems reasonable to say that this account affords an explanation, even though "only" with very high associated probability, of why gases display the uniformity expressed by Graham's law; and in physical texts and treatises, theoretical accounts of this probabilistic kind are indeed very widely referred to as explanations.

[7] The "average" velocities here referred to are technically defined as root-mean-square velocities. Their values do not differ very much from those of average velocities in the usual sense of the arithmetic mean. A succinct outline of the theoretical explanation of Graham's law can be found in Chap. 25 of Holton and Roller, *Foundations of Modern Physical Science*. The distinction, not explicitly mentioned in that presentation, between the average value of a quantity for some finite number of cases and the probabilistically estimated or expected value of that quantity is briefly discussed in Chap. 6 (especially section 4) of R. P. Feynman, R. B. Leighton, and M. Sands, *The Feynman Lectures on Physics* (Reading, Mass.: Addison-Wesley Publishing Co., 1963).

THEORIES AND

THEORETICAL EXPLANATION

6

In the preceding chapters, we have repeatedly had occasion to mention the important role that theories play in scientific explanation. We will now examine the nature and function of theories systematically, in some detail.

Theories are usually introduced when previous study of a class of phenomena has revealed a system of uniformities that can be expressed in the form of empirical laws. Theories then seek to explain those regularities and, generally, to afford a deeper and more accurate understanding of the phenomena in question. To this end, a theory construes those phenomena as manifestations of entities and processes that lie behind or beneath them, as it were. These are assumed to be governed by characteristic theoretical laws, or theoretical principles, by means of which the theory then explains the empirical uniformities that have been previously discovered, and usually also predicts "new" regularities of similar kinds. Let us consider some examples.

The Ptolemaic and Copernican systems sought to account for the observed, "apparent", motions of the heavenly bodies by means of suitable assumptions about the structure of the astronomical universe and the "actual" motions of the celestial objects. The corpuscular and the wave theories of light offered accounts of the nature of light in terms of certain underlying processes; and they explained the previously established uniformities expressed by the laws of rectilinear propagation, reflection, refraction, and diffraction as resulting from the basic laws to which the underlying processes were assumed to conform. Thus, the refraction of a beam of light passing from air into glass was explained in Huyghens' wave theory as resulting from a slowing of the light waves in the denser medium. By contrast, Newton's particle theory attributed optical refraction to a stronger attraction exerted upon the optical particles by the denser medium. Incidentally, this construal implies not only the observed bending of a beam of light: when combined with the other basic assumptions of Newton's theory, it also implies that the particles of light will be accelerated upon entering a denser medium, rather than decelerated, as the wave theory predicts. These conflicting implications were tested nearly two hundred years later by Foucault in the experiment that we briefly considered in Chapter 3, and whose outcome bore out the relevant implication of the wave theory.

To mention one more example, the kinetic theory of gases offers explanations for a wide variety of empirically established regularities by construing them as macroscopic manifestations of statistical regularities in the underlying molecular and atomic phenomena.

The basic entities and processes posited by a theory, and the laws assumed to govern them, must be specified with appropriate clarity and precision; otherwise, the theory cannot serve its scientific purpose. This important point is illustrated by the neovitalistic conception of biological phenomena. Living systems, as is well known, display a variety of striking features that seem to be distinctly purposive or teleological in character. Among them are the regeneration of lost limbs in some species; the development, in other species, of normal organisms from embryos that are damaged or even cut into several pieces in an early stage of their growth; and the remarkable coordination of the many processes in a developing organism which, as though following a common plan, lead to the formation of a mature individual. According to neovitalism, such phenomena do not occur in nonliving systems and cannot be explained by means of the concepts and laws of physics and chemistry alone; rather, they are manifestations of underlying teleological agencies of a nonphysical kind, referred to as entelechies or vital forces. Their specific mode of action is usually assumed not to violate the principles of physics and chemistry, but to direct the organic processes, within the range of possibilities left open by the physico-chemical laws, in such a way that, even in the presence of disturbing factors, embryos develop into normal individuals, and adult organisms are maintained in, or returned to, a properly functioning state.

This conception may well seem to offer us a deeper understanding of the remarkable biological phenomena in question; it may give us a sense of being more familiar, more "at home" with them. But understanding in this sense is not what is wanted in science, and a conceptual system that conveys insight into the phenomena in this intuitive sense does not for that reason alone qualify as a scientific theory. The assumptions made by a scientific theory about underlying processes must be definite enough to permit the derivation of specific implications concerning the phenomena that the theory is to explain. The neovitalistic doctrine fails on this account. It does not indicate under what circumstances entelechies will go into action and, specifically, in what way they will direct biological processes: no particular aspect of embryonic development, for example, can be inferred from the doctrine, nor does it enable us to predict what biological responses will occur under specified experimental conditions. Hence, when a new striking type of "organic directiveness" is encountered, all that the neovitalist doctrine enables us to do is to make the *post factum* pronouncement: "There is another manifestation of vital forces!"; it offers us no grounds for saying: "On the basis of the theoretical assumptions, this is just what was to be expected—the theory explains it!"

This inadequacy of the neovitalistic doctrine does not stem from the circumstance that entelechies are conceived as nonmaterial agencies, which cannot be seen or felt. This becomes clear when we contrast it with the explanation of the regularities of planetary and lunar motions by means of the Newtonian theory. Both accounts invoke nonmaterial agencies: one of them vital forces; the other, gravitational ones. But Newton's theory includes specific assumptions, expressed in the law of gravitation and the laws of motion, which determine (*a*) what gravitational forces each of a set of physical bodies of given masses and positions will exert upon the others, and (*b*) what changes in their velocities and, consequently, in their locations will be brought about by those forces. It is this characteristic that gives the theory its power to explain previously observed uniformities and also to yield predictions and retrodictions. Thus, the theory was used by Halley to predict that a comet he had observed in 1682 would return in 1759, and to identify it retrodictively with comets whose appearances had been recorded on six previous occasions, going back to the year 1066. The theory also played a spectacular explanatory and predictive role in the discovery of the planet Neptune, on the basis of irregularities in the orbit of Uranus; and subsequently in the discovery, on the basis of irregularities in Neptune's orbit, of the planet Pluto.

6.2 Internal principles and bridge principles   Broadly speaking, then, the formulation of a theory will require the specification of two kinds of principles; let us call them internal principles and bridge principles for short. The former will characterize the basic entities and processes invoked by the theory and the laws to which they are assumed to conform. The latter will indicate how the processes envisaged by the theory are related to empirical phenomena with which we are already acquainted, and which the theory may then explain, predict, or retrodict. Let us consider some examples.

In the kinetic theory of gases, the internal principles are those that characterize the "microphenomena" at the molecular level, whereas the bridge principles connect certain aspects of the microphenomena with corresponding "macroscopic" features of a gas. Consider the explanation of Graham's diffusion law, discussed in section 5.6. The internal theoretical principles it invokes include the assumptions about the random character of the molecular motions and the probabilistic laws governing them; the bridge principles include the hypothesis that the diffusion rate, a macroscopic characteristic of gas, is proportional to the average velocity of its molecules—a quantity defined in "microlevel" terms.

Or take the explanation, by the kinetic theory, of Boyle's law that the pressure of a fixed mass of gas at constant temperature is inversely proportional to its volume. This explanation invokes basically the same internal hypotheses as that of Graham's law; the connection with the macro-quantity, pressure, is established by a bridge hypothesis to the effect that the pressure exerted by a gas in a container results from the impacts of the molecules upon the containing walls and is quantitatively equal to the average value of the total momentum that the molecules deliver per second to a unit square of the wall area. These assumptions yield the conclusion that the pressure of a gas is inversely proportional to its volume and directly proportional to the mean kinetic energy of its molecules. Then, the explanation uses a second bridge hypothesis; namely, that the mean kinetic energy of the molecules of a fixed mass of gas remains constant as long as the temperature remains constant: and this principle, together with the previous conclusion, evidently yields Boyle's law.

In the examples just considered, the bridge principles may be said to connect certain theoretically assumed entities that cannot be directly observed or measured (such as moving molecules, their masses, momenta, and energies) with more or less directly observable or measurable aspects of medium-sized physical systems (e.g., the temperature or the pressure of a gas as measured by a thermometer or a pressure gauge). But bridge principles do not always connect "theoretical unobservables" with "experimental observables". This is illustrated by Bohr's explanation of the empirical generalization expressed by Balmer's formula, considered earlier, which specifies, in a readily computable form, the wavelengths of a (theoretically infinite) series of discrete lines that appear in the emission spectrum of hydrogen. Bohr's explanation is based on the assumptions that (*a*) the light emitted by electrically or thermally "excited" hydrogen vapor results from the energy released when electrons in individual atoms jump from a higher to a lower energy level; that (*b*) only a certain (theoretically infinite) set of quantitatively definite, discrete energy levels are available to the electron of a hydrogen atom; and that (*c*) the energy ΔE released by an electron jump produces light of exactly one wavelength λ, which is given by the law $\lambda = (h \cdot c)/\Delta E$, where h is Planck's constant and c is the velocity of light. As a consequence, each of the lines in the hydrogen spectrum is seen to correspond to a "quantum jump" between two specific energy levels; and from Bohr's theoretical assumptions, Balmer's formula follows indeed in quantitative detail. The internal principles here invoked include the assumptions characterizing Bohr's model of the hydrogen atom as consisting of a positive nucleus and an electron moving about it in one or another of a series of possible orbits, each corresponding to one energy level; and the assumption (*b*) above. The bridge principles, on the other hand, comprise such hypotheses as (*a*) and (*c*) above: they connect the "unobservable" theoretical entities with the subject matter to be explained—the wavelengths of certain lines in the emission spectrum of hydrogen. These wavelengths are not observables in the ordinary sense of the word, and they cannot be as simply and directly measured as, say, the length and width of a picture frame or the weight of a bag of potatoes. Their measurement is a highly indirect procedure that rests on a great many assumptions, including those of the wave theory of light. But in the context we are considering, those assumptions are taken for granted; they are presupposed even in just stating the uniformity for which a theoretical explanation is sought. Thus, the phenomena to which bridge principles link the basic entities and processes assumed by a theory need not be "directly" observable or measurable: they may well be characterized in terms of previously established theories, and their observation or measurement may presuppose the principles of those theories.

Without bridge principles, as we have seen, a theory would have no explanatory power. Without bridge principles, we may add, it would also be incapable of test. For the internal principles of a theory are concerned with the peculiar entities and processes assumed by the theory (such as the jumps of electrons from one atomic energy level to another in Bohr's theory), and they will therefore be expressed largely in terms of characteristic "theoretical concepts", which refer to those entities and processes. But the implications that permit a test of those theoretical principles will have to be expressed in terms of things and occurrences with which we are antecedently acquainted, which we already know how to observe, to measure, and to describe. In other words, while the internal principles of a theory are couched in its characteristic *theoretical terms* ('nucleus', 'orbital electron', 'energy level', 'electron jump'), the test implications must be formulated in terms (such as 'hydrogen vapor', 'emission spectrum', 'wavelength associated with a spectral line') which are "antecedently understood", as we might say, terms that have been introduced prior to the theory and can be used independently of it. Let us refer to them as *antecedently available* or *pretheoretical terms*. The derivation of such test implications from the internal principles of the theory evidently requires further premises that establish connections between the two sets of concepts; and this, as the preceding examples show, is accomplished by appropriate bridge principles (connecting, for example, the energy released in an electron jump with the wavelength of the light that is emitted as a result). Without bridge principles, the internal principles of a theory would yield no test implications, and the requirement of testability would be violated.

6.3 Theoretical understanding   Testability-in-principle and explanatory import, though crucially important, are nevertheless only minimal necessary conditions that a scientific theory must satisfy; a system that meets these requirements may yet afford little illumination and may lack scientific interest.

The distinctive characteristics of a good scientific theory cannot be stated in very precise terms. Several of them were suggested in Chapter 4, when we discussed the considerations that bear on the confirmation and acceptability of scientific hypotheses. But some additional observations are now in order.

In a field of inquiry in which some measure of understanding has already been achieved by the establishment of empirical laws, a good theory will deepen as well as broaden that understanding. First, such a theory offers a systematically unified account of quite diverse phenomena. It traces all of them back to the same underlying processes and presents the various empirical uniformities they exhibit as manifestations of one common set of basic laws. We noted earlier the great diversity of empirical regularities (such as those shown by free fall; the simple pendulum; the motions of the moon, the planets, comets, double stars, and artificial satellites; the tides, and so forth) that are accounted for by the basic principles of Newton's theory of gravitation and of motion. In similar fashion, the kinetic theory of gases exhibits a wide variety of empirical uniformities as manifestations of certain basic probabilistic uniformities in the random motions of the molecules. And Bohr's theory of the hydrogen atom accounts not only for the uniformity expressed by Balmer's formula, which refers to just one series of lines in the spectrum of hydrogen, but equally for analogous empirical laws representing the wavelengths of other series of lines in the same spectrum, including several series whose member lines lie in the invisible infrared or ultraviolet parts of the spectrum.

A theory will usually deepen our understanding also in a different way, namely by showing that the previously formulated empirical laws that it is meant to explain do not hold strictly and unexceptionally, but only approximately and within a certain limited range of application. Thus, Newton's theoretical account of planetary motion shows that Kepler's laws hold only approximately, and it explains why this is so: the Newtonian principles imply that the orbit of a planet moving about the sun under its gravitational influence alone would indeed be an ellipse, but that the gravitational pull exerted on it by other planets leads to departures from a strictly elliptical path. The theory gives a quantitative account of the resulting perturbations in terms of the masses and spatial distribution of the disturbing objects. Similarly, Newton's theory accounts for Galileo's law of free fall as simply one special manifestation of the basic laws for motion under gravitational attraction; but in so doing, it shows also that the law (even if applied to free fall in a vacuum) holds only approximately. One of the reasons is that in Galileo's formula the acceleration of free fall appears as a constant (twice the factor 16 in the formula '$s = 16t^2$'), whereas on Newton's inverse-square law of gravitational attraction, the force acting upon the falling body increases as its distance from the center of the earth decreases; hence, by virtue of Newton's second law of motion, its acceleration, too, increases in the course of the fall. Analogous remarks apply to the laws of geometrical optics as viewed from the vantage point of wave-theoretical optics. For example, even in a homogeneous medium, light does not move strictly in straight lines; it can bend around corners. And the laws of geometrical optics for reflection in curved mirrors and for image-formation by lenses hold only approximately and within certain limits.

It might therefore be tempting to say that theories often do not explain previously established laws, but refute them. But this would give a distorted picture of the insight afforded by a theory. After all a theory does not simply refute the earlier empirical generalizations in its field; rather, it shows that within a certain limited range defined by qualifying conditions, the generalizations hold true in fairly close approximation. The limited range for Kepler's laws includes those cases in which the masses of the disturbing additional planets are small compared with that of the sun, or their distances from the given planet are large compared with its distance from the sun. Similarly, the theory shows that Galileo's law holds approximately for free fall over short distances.

Finally, a good theory will also broaden our knowledge and understanding by predicting and explaining phenomena that were not known when the theory was formulated. Thus, Torricelli's conception of a sea of air led to Pascal's prediction that the column of a mercury barometer would shorten with increasing height above sea level. Einstein's general theory of relativity not only accounted for the known slow rotation of the orbit of Mercury, but also predicted the bending of light in a gravitational field, a forecast subsequently borne out by astronomical measurements. Maxwell's theory of electromagnetism implied the existence of electromagnetic waves and predicted important characteristics of their propagation. Those implications, too, were later confirmed by the experimental work of Heinrich Hertz, and they provided the basis for the technology of radio transmission, among other applications.

Such striking predictive successes will of course greatly strengthen our confidence in a theory that already has given us a systematically unified explanation—and often also a correction—of previously established laws. The insight that such a theory gives us is much deeper than that afforded by empirical laws; and it is widely held, therefore, that a scientifically adequate explanation of a class of empirical phenomena can be achieved only by means of an appropriate theory. Indeed, it seems to be a remarkable fact that even if we limited ourselves to a study of the more or less directly observable or measurable aspects of our world and tried to explain these, in the manner discussed in Chapter 5, by means of laws couched in terms of observables, our efforts would have only limited success. For the laws that are formulated at the observational level generally turn out to hold only approximately and within a limited range; whereas by theoretical recourse to entities and events under the familiar surface, a much more comprehensive and exact account can be achieved. It is intriguing to speculate whether simpler worlds are conceivable where all phenomena are at the observable surface, so to speak; where there occur perhaps only changes of color and of shape, within a finite range of possibilities, and strictly in accordance with some simple laws of universal form.

6.4 The status of theoretical entities   At any rate, the natural sciences have achieved their deepest and most far-reaching insights by descending below the level of familiar empirical phenomena; and it is hardly surprising, therefore, that some thinkers consider the underlying structures, forces, and processes assumed by well-established theories as the only real constituents of the world. This is the view expressed by Eddington in the provocative Introduction to his book, *The Nature of the Physical World*. Eddington begins by telling his readers that, in settling down to write his book, he drew up his two chairs to his two tables; and he goes on to expound the differences between the tables:

One of them has been familiar to me from earliest years. . . . It has extension; it is comparatively permanent; it is coloured; above all it is *substantial* . . . Table No. 2 is my scientific table. It . . . is mostly emptiness. Sparsely scattered in that emptiness are numerous electric charges rushing about with great speed; but their combined bulk amounts to less than a billionth of the bulk of the table itself. [Nevertheless, it] supports my writing paper as satisfactorily as table No. 1; for when I lay the paper on it the little electric particles with their headlong speed keep on hitting the underside, so that the paper is maintained in shuttlecock fashion at a nearly steady level. . . . It makes all the difference in the world whether the paper before me is poised as it were on a swarm of flies . . . , or whether it is supported because there is substance below it, it being the intrinsic nature of substance to occupy space to the exclusion of other substance. . . . I need not tell you that modern physics has by delicate test and remorseless logic assured me that my second scientific table is the only one which is really there . . . On the other hand I need not tell you that modern physics will never succeed in exorcising that first table—strange compound of external nature, mental imagery and inherited prejudice—which lies visible to my eyes and tangible to my grasp.[1]

But this conception, however persuasively presented, is untenable; for to explain a phenomenon is not to explain it away. It is neither the aim nor the effect of theoretical explanations to show that the familiar things and events of our everyday experience are not "really there". The kinetic theory of gases plainly does not show that there are no such things as macroscopic bodies of different gases that change volumes under changing pressure, diffuse through porous walls at characteristic rates, etc., and that there "really" are only swarms of randomly buzzing molecules. On the contrary, the theory takes for granted that there are those macroscopic events and uniformities, and it seeks to account for them in terms of the microstructure of the gases and the microprocesses involved in their various changes. That the macrophenomena are presupposed by the theory is clearly shown by the fact that its bridge principles make explicit reference to certain macroscopic characteristics —such as pressure, volume, temperature, diffusion rate—which are associated with macro-objects and macroprocesses. Similarly, the atomic theory of matter does not show that a table is not a substantial, solid, hard object; it takes these things for granted and seeks to show in virtue of what aspects of the underlying microprocesses a table displays those macroscopic characteristics. In so doing, the theory may, of

---

[1] A. S. Eddington, *The Nature of the Physical World* (New York: Cambridge University Press, 1929), pp. ix-xii (italics in the original); quoted by kind permission of Cambridge University Press.

course, reveal as mistaken certain particular notions we might have entertained about the nature of a body of gas or of a solid object, such as perhaps the notion that such physical bodies are thoroughly homogeneous, no matter how small the parts of them that might be considered; but correcting misconceptions of this kind is a far cry from showing that everyday objects and their familiar characteristics are not "really there".

Some scientists and philosophers of science have taken a view diametrically opposite to that just considered. Broadly speaking, they deny the existence of "theoretical entities" or regard theoretical assumptions about them as ingeniously contrived fictions, which afford a formally simple and convenient descriptive and predictive account of observable things and events. This general view has been held in several rather different forms, and on different grounds.

One type of consideration, which has been influential in recent philosophical studies of the issue, can be briefly stated as follows: if a proposed theory is to have a clear meaning, then surely the new theoretical concepts that are used in its formulation must be clearly and objectively defined in terms of concepts that are already available and understood. But as a rule, such full definitions are not provided in the customary formulation of a theory; and closer logical examination of the way in which new theoretical concepts are connected with antecedently available concepts suggests that such definitions may indeed be unattainable. But, so the argument continues, a theory expressed in terms of such inadequately characterized concepts must then in turn lack fully definite meaning: its principles, which purport to speak about certain theoretical entities and occurrences, are, strictly, no definite statements at all; they are neither true nor false; at best they form a convenient and effective symbolic apparatus for inferring certain empirical phenomena (such as the appearance of characteristic lines in a suitably placed spectrograph) from others (such as the passing of an electric discharge through hydrogen gas).

The ways in which the meanings of scientific terms are specified will be examined more closely in the following chapter. For the moment, let us note only that the demand for full definition, on which this argument is based, is overly stringent. It is possible to make clear and precise use of a concept for which no full definition, but only a partial specification of meaning, has been provided. For example, a characterization of the concept of temperature by reference to the readings of a mercury thermometer affords no general definition of temperature; it assigns no temperature below the freezing point or above the boiling point of mercury. Yet, within these limits, the concept can be used in a precise and objective fashion. Moreover, the range of its applicability can be expanded by specifying alternative ways of measuring temperatures. Or consider the principle that the inertial masses of physical bodies are inversely proportional to the accelerations imparted upon them by equal forces. Again, this formulation does not fully define what is meant by the mass of a given body; and yet it affords a partial characterization that permits a test of certain statements couched in terms of the concept of mass. The bridge principles of a theory similarly provide partial criteria, expressed in terms of antecedently understood concepts, for the use of theoretical terms. Hence, the lack of full definitions can hardly justify the conception of theoretical terms, and of the theoretical principles containing them, as mere symbolic computation devices.

A second, quite different, argument against the existence of theoretical entities proceeds as follows: Any body of empirical findings, however rich and diverse, can in principle be subsumed under many different laws or theories. Thus, if a set of experimentally determined pairs of associated values of an "independent" and a "dependent" physical variable are represented by points in a graph, then, as we saw earlier, the points can be connected by many different curves; and each of these will represent one tentative law that accounts for the associated pairs that have so far been measured. An analogous remark holds for theories. But when two alternative theories—such as the particle and the wave theories of light before the "crucial experiments" of the nineteenth century—equally account for a given set of empirical phenomena, then, if "real existence" is granted to the theoretical entities assumed by one of them, it must be granted as well to the quite different entities assumed by the other; hence, the entities posited by none of the alternative theories can be held actually to exist.

This argument, however, would oblige us to say also that when we seem to hear a bird singing outside the open window, we must not assume that there really is a bird, since the sound could be accounted for also by the alternative hypothesis that someone was blowing a bird whistle. But clearly, there are ways of finding out which, if either, of these assumptions is correct; for apart from explaining the sound we heard, the two accounts have further, different, implications that we can test if we want to find out whether it was "really" a bird or a whistle or still something else that produced the sound. Similarly, as we saw earlier, the two optical theories have further differentiating implications by which they can be, and have been, tested. The gradual elimination of some among the conceivable alternative hypotheses or theories can never, it is true, narrow the field of competitors to the point where only one of them is left; hence, we can never establish *with certainty* that a given theory is true, that the entities it posits are real. But to say that is not to disclose a peculiar flaw in our claims about theoretical entities, but to note a pervasive characteristic of *all* empirical knowledge.

A third argument that has been adduced against assuming the existence of theoretical entities is, briefly, to this effect: scientific inquiry is aimed, in the last analysis, at providing a systematic and coherent account of the "facts", of the phenomena we encounter in our sense experience; and its explanatory assumptions should, strictly, refer only to entities and processes that are at least potential facts, potentially accessible to our senses. Hypotheses and theories that purport to go essentially behind the phenomena of our experience can at best be useful formal devices but cannot claim to represent aspects of the physical world. On grounds of this kind, the eminent physicist-philosopher Ernst Mach, among others, held that the atomic theory of matter provided a mathematical model for the representation of certain facts, but that no physical "reality" could be claimed for atoms or molecules.

We have noted, however, that if science were thus to limit itself to the study of observable phenomena, it would hardly be able to formulate any precise and general explanatory laws at all, whereas quantitively precise and comprehensive explanatory principles can be formulated in terms of underlying entities such as molecules, atoms, and subatomic particles. And since such theories are tested and confirmed in basically the same way as hypotheses couched in terms of more or less directly observable or measurable things and events, it seems arbitrary to reject theoretically postulated entities as fictitious.

But is there not an important difference, after all, between these two levels? Suppose we wish to explain the performance of a given "black box", which responds to different kinds of input by specific and complex outputs. We might then venture a hypothesis about the internal structure of the box—perhaps in terms of wheels, gears, and ratchets, or in terms of wires, vacuum tubes, and currents. Such a hypothesis might be tested by varying the inputs and checking the corresponding outputs; by listening to noises coming from the box, and the like. But there remains also the possibility of opening the box and checking the hypothesis by direct inspection; for the components assumed in the hypothesis are all macroscopic and, in principle, accessible to observation. When, on the other hand, the input-output connection between pressure changes and associated volume changes of a gas at constant temperature are explained in terms of molecular micromechanisms, no such test by observation is possible.

But the distinction here suggested is not as clear and as telling as it might seem, for the class of observables it refers to is not very precisely delimited. Presumably it should include all those things, properties, and processes whose presence or occurrence can be ascertained by normal human observers "immediately", without the mediation of special instruments or of interpretative hypotheses or theories. The wheels, gears, and ratchets of our example would belong to this class, and so would their interlocking movements. Similarly, wires and switches might be counted as observable. But doubts would arise concerning the status of things such as vacuum tubes. Undeniably, a vacuum tube is a physical object that can be "directly" seen and felt; but when we refer to it as a vacuum tube (as we would in explaining the output of the black box), we describe that object as having a certain complex property (namely, a characteristic physical structure); and we must ask therefore, whether an object is observable "under that description", whether the property of being a vacuum tube is of a kind whose presence in a given case can be ascertained by immediate observation. Now in order to determine whether a given object is a vacuum tube, we may sometimes simply see whether it looks like one, but for a more dependable decision—especially on whether the object is a properly working vacuum tube, as assumed in the black-box example—various physical tests would be required; these would make use of instruments, and the interpretation of the instrument readings would presuppose a host of physical laws and theoretical principles. But if the characterization of an object as a vacuum tube must be counted as going beyond the realm of observables, then the black-box example loses its force.

Let us pursue the argument in a somewhat different direction. Wires strung in the black box, we said, might count as observables. But we would surely not want to say that a rather fine wire becomes a fictitious entity when weakening eyesight compels us to use glasses to see it. But then, it would be arbitrary to disqualify objects, such as extremely fine wires or threads, or small specks of dust, that no human observer can see without a magnifying glass. By the same token, we will have to admit objects that can be observed only with the aid of a microscope, and so on down to objects that can be observed only by means of Geiger counters, bubble chambers, electron miscroscopes, and other such devices.

Thus, there is a gradual transition from the macroscopic objects of our everyday experience to bacteria, viruses, molecules, atoms, and subatomic particles; and any line drawn to divide them into actual physical objects and fictitious entities would be quite arbitrary.[2]

[2] Our discussion of the status of theoretical entities has been limited to a consideration of some important basic issues. A fuller and more penetrating study, and references to further literature, will be found in Chaps.5 and 6 of E. Nagel, *The Structure of Science*. Another very stimulating work dealing with these issues is J.J.C. Smart, *Philosophy and Scientific Realism* (London: Routledge and Kegan Paul Ltd.; New York: The Humanities Press, 1963).

It is sometimes said that scientific explanations effect a reduction of a puzzling, and often unfamiliar, phenomenon to facts and principles with which we are already familiar. And no doubt this characterization fits some explanations quite well. The wave-theoretical explanations of previously established optical laws, the explanations offered by the kinetic theory of gases, and even Bohr's models of the atoms of hydrogen and the other elements—all invoke certain ideas with which we are acquainted through their use in the description and explanation of familiar phenomena, such as the propagation of water waves, the motions and collisions of billiard balls, the orbital motion of the planets about the sun. Some writers, such as the physicist N. R. Campbell, have maintained that a scientific theory that is to be of any value at all must "display an analogy": the basic laws that its internal principles specify for the theoretical entities and processes must be "analogous to some known laws", as the laws for the propagation of light waves are analogous to (have the same mathematical form as) the propagation of water waves.

However, the view that an adequate scientific explanation must, in a more or less precise sense, effect a reduction to the familiar, does not stand up under close examination. To begin with, this view would seem to imply the idea that phenomena with which we are already familiar are not in need of, or perhaps incapable of, scientific explanation; whereas in fact, science does seek to explain such "familiar" phenomena as the regular sequence of day and night and of the seasons, the phases of the moon, lightning and thunder, the color patterns of rainbows and of oil slicks, and the observation that coffee and milk, or white and black sand, when stirred or shaken, will mix, but never unmix again. Scientific explanation is not aimed at creating a sense of at-homeness or of familiarity with the phenomena of nature. That kind of feeling may well be evoked even by metaphorical accounts that have no explanatory value at all, such as the "natural affinity" construal of gravitation or the conception of biological processes as being directed by vital forces. What scientific explanation, especially theoretical explanation, aims at is not this intuitive and highly subjective kind of understanding, but an objective kind of insight that is achieved by a systematic unification, by exhibiting the phenomena as manifestations of common underlying structures and processes that conform to specific, testable, basic principles. If such an account can be given in terms that show certain analogies with familiar phenomena, then very well.

Otherwise, science will not hesitate to explain even the familiar by reduction to the unfamiliar, by means of concepts and principles of novel kinds that may at first be repugnant to our intuition. This has happened, for example, in the theory of relativity with its startling implications concerning the relativity of length, mass, temporal duration, and simultaneity; and in quantum mechanics with its principle of uncertainty and its renunciation of a strictly causal conception of the processes involving individual elementary particles.

CONCEPT FORMATION

7

Scientific statements are typically formulated in special terms, such as 'mass', 'force', 'magnetic field', 'entropy', 'phase space', and so forth. If those terms are to serve their purpose, their meanings will have to be so specified as to make sure that the resulting statements are properly testable and that they lend themselves to use in explanations, predictions, and retrodictions. In this chapter, we shall consider how this is done.

It will be helpful for our purposes to distinguish clearly between *concepts*, such as those of mass, force, magnetic field, etc., and the corresponding *terms*, the verbal or symbolic expressions that stand for those concepts. To refer to particular terms, just as to refer to particular things of any other kind, we need names or designations for them. In accordance with a standard convention of logic and analytic philosophy, we form a name or designation for a term by placing single quotes around it. Accordingly, we speak of the terms 'mass', 'force', etc., as we have already done in the first sentence of this section. We will be concerned, then, in this chapter, with methods of specifying the meanings of scientific terms and with the requirements those methods have to meet.

Definition may seem the most obvious, and perhaps the only adequate, method of characterizing a scientific concept. Let us consider this procedure. Definitions are offered for one or the other of two quite different purposes, namely:

a] to state or describe the accepted meaning, or meanings, of a term already in use;

b] to assign, by stipulation, a special meaning to a given term, which may be a newly coined verbal or symbolic expression (such as 'pi-meson') or an "old" term that is to be used in a specific technical sense (e.g., the term 'strangeness' as used in the theory of elementary particles).

Definitions serving the first purpose will be called *descriptive*; those serving the second purpose will be called *stipulative*.

Definitions of the first kind can be stated in the form

——— has the same meaning as — — —

The term to be defined, or the *definiendum*, occupies the place of the solid line on the left, while the place of the broken line is occupied by the defining expression, or the *definiens*. Here are some examples of such descriptive definitions:

'Father' has the same meaning as 'male parent'.
'Appendicitis' has the same meaning as 'inflammation of the appendix'.
'Simultaneous' has the same meaning as 'occurring at the same time'.

Definitions such as these purport to analyze the accepted meaning of a term and to describe it with the help of other terms—whose meaning must be antecedently understood if the definition is to serve its purpose. They will therefore also be called descriptive definitions, and more specifically, *analytic definitions*. In the next chapter, we will consider statements that may be viewed as descriptive definitions of a nonanalytic kind: they specify the range of application, or extension, of a term, rather than its meaning, or intension. Descriptive definitions of either kind claim to describe certain aspects of the accepted use of a term; they may, therefore, be said to be more or less accurate, and even true or false.

Stipulative definitions, on the other hand, serve to introduce an expression that is to be used in some specific sense in the context of a discussion, or a theory, or the like. Such definitions can be given the form

——— is to have the same meaning as — — —
or
By ——— let us understand the same thing as by — — —

The expressions on the left and right are again called the definiendum and the definiens, respectively. The resulting definitions have the character of stipulations or conventions, which evidently cannot be qualified as true or false. The following examples illustrate ways in which such definitions might be formulated in scientific writings; each of them can readily be put into one of the standard forms just cited.

Let us use the term 'acholia' as short for 'lack of secretion of bile'. The term 'density' is to be short for 'mass in grams per cubic centimeter'.

By an acid we will understand an electrolyte that furnishes hydrogen ions.

Particles of charge zero and mass number one will be called neutrons.

A term defined by an analytic or a stipulative definition can always be eliminated from a sentence by substituting its definiens for it: this procedure turns the sentence into an equivalent one that no longer contains the term. For example, on one of the definitions just formulated, the sentence 'The density of gold is greater than that of lead' can be translated into 'A cubic centimeter of gold has a greater mass in grams than the same volume of lead.' In this sense, as Quine has put it, to define a term is to show how to avoid it.

The injunction 'Define your terms!' has the ring of a sound scientific maxim; indeed, it may seem that ideally, every term used in a scientific theory or in a given branch of science should be precisely defined. But that is logically impossible; for having formulated a definition for one term, we would then have to define in turn each of the terms used in the definiens, and then the terms used to define any of the latter, and so forth. But in the resulting chains of definitions, we must avoid "circles" defining a term with the help of some of its predecessors in the chain. Such a circle is illustrated by the following string of definitions, in which the phrase 'is to have the same meaning as' is replaced by the abbreviatory symbol '$=_{Df}$':

> 'parent' $=_{Df}$ 'father or mother'
> 'father' $=_{Df}$ 'male parent'
> 'mother' $=_{Df}$ 'parent, but not father'

To determine the meaning of 'father', we would replace the term 'parent' in the second definition by its definiens as specified in the first. But this yields the expression 'male (father or mother)', which defines the term 'father' by means of itself (and of other terms), and thus falls short of its purpose; for it does not enable us to avoid the defined word. Similar troubles arises from the third definition. The only way of escaping this difficulty in our attempt to define *every* term of a given system is never to use a term in a definiens that has been defined earlier in the chain. But then, our chain of definitions will never end; for however far we may have gone, the terms used in the last definiens remain to be defined since, on our assumption, they have not been defined before. Such an infinite regress would, of course, be self-defeating: our understanding of one term would depend on that of the next one, which would depend on that of the next one, and so on indefinitely, with the result that no term would ever be explained.

Not every term in a scientific system, therefore, can be defined by means of other terms of the system: there will have to be a set of so-called primitive terms, which receive no definitions within the system, and which serve as a basis for defining all the other terms. This is very clearly taken into account in the axiomatic formulation of mathematical theories. In each of the different modern axiomatizations of Euclidean geometry, for example, a list of primitive terms is explicitly specified, and all other terms are introduced by chains of stipulative definitions that lead back to expressions containing only primitive terms.[1]

Consider now the terms used in a scientific theory. In accordance with the distinction suggested in Chapter 6, we will think of them as divided into two classes: theoretical terms proper, which are characteristic of the theory, and pretheoretical, or antecedently available, terms. How are the meanings of the theoretical terms specified? Let us note first that just as in a purely mathematical theory, so also in a scientific one, some of the theoretical terms can be defined by means of others. In mechanics, the instantaneous velocity and acceleration of a point mass are defined as the first and the second derivatives of the location of the point mass, taken as a function of time; in atomic theory, a deuteron can be defined as a nucleus of that isotope of hydrogen whose mass number is 2; and so forth. But while such definitions serve an important purpose in the formulation and use of a theory, they clearly do not suffice to instill definite empirical content into the defined terms, and thus to make them applicable to empirical subject matter. For that purpose, we need statements that specify the meanings of theoretical terms by means of expressions that are already understood and can be used without reference to the theory. What we have called the pretheoretical terms serve precisely this purpose. We will use the term '*interpretative sentence*' to refer to statements that thus specify the meanings of the theoretical terms proper, or of the "characteristic terms", of a given theory by means of its antecedently available, or pretheoretical vocabulary. Let us now examine the character of such sentences more closely.

7.2 Operational definitions   A very specific conception of the character of interpretative sentences has been put forward by the operationist school of thought, which grew out of the methodological work of the physicist P. W. Bridgman.[2] The central idea of operationism is that the meaning of every scientific term must be specifiable by indicating a definite testing operation that provides a criterion for its application. Such criteria are

---

[1] Fuller details on this point will be found in another volume of this series: S. Barker, *Philosophy of Mathematics*, pp. 22-26, 40-41.

[2] Bridgman's first, and now classical, presentation is given in his book, *The Logic of Modern Physics* (New York: The Macmillan Company, 1927).

often referred to as "operational definitions". Whether they are definitions in a strict sense is a question that we shall consider later. First, we shall look at some examples.

In an early stage of chemical inquiry, the term 'acid' might be "operationally defined" as follows: in order to ascertain whether the term 'acid' applies to a given liquid—i.e., whether the liquid is an acid— insert a strip of blue litmus paper into it; the liquid is an acid if and only if the litmus paper turns red. This criterion indicates a definite *testing operation*, inserting blue litmus paper, for finding out whether the term applies to a given liquid, and it states a specific *test result* (the paper turning red) that is to count as indicating that the term applies to the given liquid.

Similarly, the term 'harder than' as applied to minerals, might be operationally characterized as follows: to determine whether mineral m_1 is harder than mineral m_2, draw a sharp point of a piece of m_1 under pressure across the surface of a piece of m_2 (test operation); m_1 will be said to be harder than m_2 just in case a scratch is produced (specific test result).

Some definitions that make no explicit mention of operations and outcomes can readily be thrown into the form of an operational specification. Take this characterization of a magnet: A bar of iron or steel is called a magnet if iron filings are attracted by its ends and cling to them. An explicitly operationist version would read: to find out whether the term 'magnet' applies to a given iron or steel bar, put iron filings close to it. If the filings are attracted by the ends of the bar and cling to them, the bar is a magnet.

The terms considered in our three examples—'acid', 'harder than', 'magnet'—were here construed as standing for nonquantitative concepts; the operational criteria, accordingly, made no provision for *degrees* of acidity or hardness, or for strength of magnetization. The operationist maxim, however, is definitely meant to apply as well to the characterization of terms such as 'length', 'mass', 'velocity', 'temperature', 'electric charge', and the like, which stand for quantitative concepts admitting of numerical values. Here, operational definition is conceived as specifying a procedure for determining the numerical value of the given quantity in particular cases: operational definitions take on the character of rules of measurement.

Thus, an operational definition of 'length' might specify a procedure involving the use of rigid measuring rods for determining the length of the distance between two points; an operational definition of 'temperature' might specify how the temperature of a body—e.g., a liquid— is to be determined by means of a mercury thermometer, and so on.

The operational procedure invoked in any operational definition must be so chosen that it can be unequivocally carried out by any competent observer, and that the result can be objectively ascertained and does not essentially depend on who performs the test. Thus, in defining the term 'aesthetic merit' in reference to paintings, it would not be permissible to use this operational instruction: contemplate the painting and note that place on a point scale from 1 to 10 that seems to you best to indicate the beauty of the painting.

One purpose of the operationist insistence on unequivocal operational criteria of application for all scientific terms is to insure objective testability for all scientific statements. Consider, for example, the following hypothesis: 'The brittleness of ice increases with decreasing temperature; or more precisely, of any two pieces of ice of different temperature, the one with the lower temperature is brittler than the other.' Suppose that adequate operational procedures have been specified for determining whether a given substance is ice, and for measuring, or at last comparing, the temperatures of different pieces of ice. Then the hypothesis still has no clear meaning—it does not yield definite test implications—unless clear criteria are also available for the comparison of brittleness. The fact that such phrases as 'brittler than' or 'increasing brittleness' seem to be intuitively clear does not suffice to make them acceptable for scientific use. But if a clear-cut operational rule of application for these terms is provided, the hypothesis becomes indeed testable in the sense we considered earlier. Thus, properly chosen operational criteria of application for a set of terms will insure the testability of the statements in which they occur.[3]

Correlatively, operationists argue, the use of terms that lack operational definitions—no matter how intuitively clear and familiar they may seem—leads to meaningless statements and questions. Thus, the claim we considered earlier that gravitational attraction is due to an underlying natural affinity would be declared meaningless because no operational criteria for the concept of natural affinity have been provided. Similarly, in the absence of operational criteria of absolute motion, the question whether the earth or the sun (or both) are "really" moving is rejected as a meaningless question.[4]

These basic ideas of operationism have exerted considerable influence on methodological thinking in psychology and the social sciences,

---

[3] This claim is subject to certain qualifications concerning the logical form of the statements in question, but these may be passed over in this general discussion of operationism.

[4] In this connection, sections 3 and 4 of Chap. 13 in Holton and Roller, *Foundations of Modern Physical Science*, provide interesting further illustrations and comments. And the reader may find it stimulating to examine, from the vantage points of operationism and of the requirement of testability, the scientific significance of the intriguing questions that Bridgman offers for consideration near the end of Chap. 1 of *The Logic of Modern Physics*.

where great emphasis has been placed on the need to provide clear operational criteria for terms that are to serve in hypotheses or theories. Hypotheses such as that more intelligent people tend to be emotionally less stable than their less intelligent fellows, or that mathematical ability is strongly correlated with musical ability, cannot be objectively tested unless clear criteria of application for the constituent terms are available. A vague intuitive understanding does not suffice for the purpose, though it may suggest ways of specifying objective criteria.

In psychology, such criteria are usually formulated in terms of *tests* (of intelligence, emotional stability, mathematical ability, and so forth). Broadly speaking, the operational procedure consists in administering the test according to specifications; the test results consist in the responses of the subjects tested, or, as a rule, in some qualitative or quantitative summary or evaluation of those responses, obtained by a procedure that may be more or less objective and more or less precise. The evaluation of a subject's responses in a Rorschach test, for example, relies more heavily on the interpreter's gradually acquired competence in judgment and less on precise explicit criteria than does the Stanford-Binet test for intelligence; and the Rorschach is, therefore, less satisfactory than the Stanford-Binet, from the operationist point of view. Some of the principal objections that have been raised against psychoanalytic theorizing concern the lack of adequate criteria of application for psychoanalytic terms, and the concomitant difficulties in deriving unequivocal test implications from the hypotheses in which they function.

The warnings thus posted by operationism have been distinctly stimulating for the philosophical and methodological study of science. They have also exerted a strong influence on research procedures in psychology and the social sciences. But as we shall now see, a too restrictive operationist construal of the empirical character of science has tended to obscure the systematic and theoretical aspects of scientific concepts and the strong interdependence of concept formation and theory formation.

7.3 Empirical and systematic import of scientific concepts

Operationism holds that the meaning of a term is fully and exclusively determined by its operational definition. Thus, Bridgman says: "The concept of length is therefore fixed when the operations by which length is measured are fixed: that is, the concept of length involves as much as and nothing more than the set of operations by which length is determined. In general, we mean by any concept nothing more than a set of operations; *the concept is synonymous with the corresponding set of operations.*" [5] This view im-

---

[5] Bridgman, *The Logic of Modern Physics*, p. 5 (Bridgman's italics).

plies that a scientific term has meaning only within the range of those empirical situations in which the operational procedure "defining" it can be performed. Suppose, for example, that we develop physics from scratch, so to speak, and introduce the term "length" by reference to the operation of measuring the length of rectilinear distances with a rigid measuring rod. Then no meaning has been attached to the question 'How long is the circumference of this cylinder?' or to statements offering an answer to it, for the operation of measuring length with straight rigid rods is evidently inapplicable in this case. If the concept of length is to have a definite meaning in this context, then a new and different operational criterion must be specified. This might be done by stipulating that the circumference of a cylinder is to be measured by tightly fitting a flexible inextensible tape around it, and then straightening the tape and measuring its length with a rigid rod. Similarly, our initial method of measuring length cannot be used to determine the distances of extraterrestrial objects; and operationism tells us that if statements about such distances are to have a definite meaning, appropriate measuring operations must be specified. One of these might be an optical method of triangulation similar to that used in surveying for the determination of certain terrestrial distances; another one might involve bouncing back a radar signal at the extraterrestrial object and measuring the elapsed time.

The choice of such additional operational criteria will naturally be subject to this important condition, which might be called the *requirement of consistency*: whenever two different procedures are applicable, they must yield the same results. For example, if the distance between two markers on a building lot is determined by means of rigid rods and by optical triangulation, the numerical values thus obtained should be the same. Or suppose that a temperature scale is first "operationally defined" by the readings of a mercury thermometer and is then to be extended downwards by using alcohol, with its much lower freezing point, as a thermometric liquid: then it must be made sure that, within the range where both kinds of thermometer can be used, they give the same readings.

But at this point, Bridgman introduces a further consideration. The finding that, within the range of their common applicability, two measuring operations yield the same results has the character of an empirical generalization; hence, even if it has been borne out in careful tests, it may conceivably be false. For this reason, Bridgman holds, it would not be "safe" to regard the two operational procedures as determining one and the same concept: different operational criteria should be regarded as characterizing different concepts; and these should, ideally, be referred to by different terms. Thus, the terms 'tactual length' and 'optical length' might be used to refer to the quantities determined with the help of measuring rods and of optical triangulation, respectively. Similarly, we would have to distinguish between mercury-temperature and alcohol-temperature.

But as we shall now see, this drastic conclusion is hardly warranted by the supporting argument, which overemphasizes the need for an unequivocal empirical interpretation of scientific terms and does not take adequate account of what we shall call their systematic import. Suppose that, following Bridgman's maxim, we distinguish tactual and optical length and after careful tests, establish a putative law to the effect that for any physical interval to which both measuring procedures are applicable, the two lengths have the same numerical value. If we should subsequently discover conditions under which the two procedures yield different results, we would have to abandon our putative law, but we could continue to use the terms 'tactual length' and 'optical length' without changing their meanings.

But what would the discovery of such cases of disagreement entail if, contrary to Bridgman's maxim, the two operational procedures were construed as different ways of measuring one and the same quantity, referred to simply as "length"? Since the requirement of consistency for the two procedures would be violated, one of the criteria would have to be abandoned: we could continue to use the term 'length', but with a modified operational interpretation.

Thus, an adjustment to discordant empirical findings could be made in either case, either by abandoning a tentatively accepted law or by modifying the operational interpretation of a term.

In addition—and this is a much more serious objection—it would be difficult, indeed impossible, strictly to adhere to Bridgman's maxim. As a body of laws and eventually of theoretical principles is gradually established in a field of inquiry, its concepts become linked in various ways to each other and to previously available concepts. Such linkages often provide quite new "operational" criteria of application. Thus, laws linking the resistance of a metal wire to its temperature permit the construction of a resistance thermometer; the law connecting the temperature of a gas at constant pressure with its volume is the basis for a gas thermometer; the thermoelectric effect permits the construction of a temperature-measuring device called a thermel; an optical pyrometer determines the temperature of very hot bodies by measuring the brightness of the associated radiation they emit. Similarly, laws and theoretical principles afford a large variety of ways for measuring distances. Thus, the lawful decrease of barometric pressure with altitude is the basis for barometric altimeters in airplanes; underwater distances are frequently measured by determining the traveling time of sound signals; small astronomical distances are measured by optical triangulation or by radar signals; the distance of globular star clusters and of galactic systems is inferred, by laws, from the period and the apparent brightness of certain variable stars in those systems. The measurement of very small distances may involve the use, and presuppose the theory, of optical microscopes, electron microscopes, spectrographic procedures, X-ray diffraction methods, and many others. The maxim suggested by Bridgman would oblige us to distinguish a corresponding variety of concepts of temperature and of length. And the lists would be far from complete; for even the use of two barometers of somewhat different construction, in measuring altitudes—or of two different microscopes in determining the length of bacteria—would strictly have to count as determining two different kinds, or concepts, of length, since the operational details would differ to some extent. Thus, the operationist maxim under discussion would oblige us to countenance a proliferation of concepts of length, of temperature, and of all other scientific concepts that would not only be practically unmanageable, but theoretically endless. And this would defeat one of the principal purposes of science; namely the attainment of a simple, systematically unified account of empirical phenomena.

Scientific systematization requires the establishment of diverse connections, by laws or theoretical principles, between different aspects of the empirical world, which are characterized by scientific concepts. Thus, the concepts of science are the knots in a network of systematic interrelationships in which laws and theoretical principles form the threads. The laws that form the basis of the different thermometric methods illustrate some of the "nomic threads" connecting the concept of temperature with other knot-concepts. The more threads converge upon, or issue from, a conceptual knot, the stronger will be its systematizing role, or its systematic import. Moreover, simplicity in the sense of economy of concepts is an important feature of a good scientific theory; and broadly speaking, the systematic import of the concepts in a theoretically economic system may be said to be stronger than that of the concepts in a less economic theory for the same subject matter.

Thus, considerations of systematic import militate strongly against the proliferation of concepts called for by the maxim that different operational criteria determine different concepts. And indeed, in scientific theorizing we do not find the distinction between numerous different concepts of length (for example), each characterized by its own operational definition. Rather, physical theory envisages one basic concept of length and various more or less accurate ways of measuring lengths in different circumstances. Theoretical considerations will often indicate within what domain a method of measurement is applicable, and with what accuracy.

Besides, the development of a system of laws—and especially of a theory—often leads to a modification of the operational criteria originally adopted for some of the central concepts. For example, an operational characterization of length will have to specify a unit of measurement, among other things. One standard way of doing this is to designate the distance between two marks engraved on a particular metal bar as defining the unit. But physical laws and theoretical principles then show that the distance between the marks will vary with the temperature of the bar and with any stresses that may affect it. To insure a uniform standard of length, certain further conditions are therefore added to the initial definition. The meter, for example, is defined by the distance of two marks engraved upon the International Prototype Meter, a bar made of platinum-iridium alloy, with a peculiar X-like cross section: the marks are said, by definitional convention, to have a distance of one meter when the bar is at the temperature of melting ice and is symmetrically supported by two rollers at right angles to its length and .571 meters apart in a horizontal plane. The peculiar cross section is designed to insure maximal rigidity of the bar; the specifications about its mode of support are prompted by the consideration that sagging will slightly modify the distance between the marks; and theoretical analysis shows the prescribed placement of the rollers to be optimal in the sense that slight changes in their location will leave the distance of the marks virtually unaffected.[6]

Let us consider one further example. One of the earliest and most important empirical criteria for the measurement of time was provided by the uniformities in the apparent motions of the sun and the fixed stars: the time that elapsed between two successive appearances of a celestial object in the same apparent position (e.g., of the sun in its zenith position) marked a unit of time. Smaller units were "operationally" characterized by means of sundials, sand clocks, water clocks, and later by pendulum clocks. Note that at this stage it makes no sense to ask whether two different solar days or two different full swings of a given pendulum "really" are of equal temporal duration. Operationism rightly reminds us that since, at this stage, the specified criteria serve to *define* equal duration, the question whether the temporal periods marked off by them are equal can receive only the trivial answer: yes—

---

[6] An account of the details and of the underlying theoretical considerations can be found in Norman Feather, *Mass, Length and Time* (Baltimore, Maryland: Penguin Books, 1961), Chap. 2.

by definitional convention. To assert their equality is not to make a statement of empirical fact about which we might be mistaken.

But as physical laws and theories involving the concept of time are formulated and gradually refined, they may lead to a modification of the initial operational criteria. Thus, classical mechanics implies that the period of a pendulum is dependent on its amplitude; and the heliocentric theory, which accounts for the apparent motions of celestial objects by the daily axial rotation of the earth and its annual revolution about the sun, implies, when combined with Newtonian theory, that different solar days are not of equal temporal duration even if the earth rotates at an unchanging rate. But tidal friction and similar factors give reason to assume that the daily rotation of the earth should actually be decelerating very slowly, an assumption supported by comparing the reported time of occurrence of certain solar eclipses in antiquity with the times retrodictively computed from present astronomical data. Thus, the processes originally used for the measurement of time come to be treated as affording only approximately correct measures; and eventually, new and quite different systems—such as quartz clocks and atomic clocks—come to be adopted, on theoretical grounds, as providing more accurate time scales.

But how can laws or theories show the inaccuracy of the operational criteria for the very terms in which they are formulated—criteria that must be presupposed and used in testing the laws or theories in question? The process might be compared to building a bridge across a river by putting it first on pontoons or on temporary supports sunk into the river bottom, then using the bridge as a platform for improving and perhaps even shifting the foundations, and then again adjusting and expanding the superstructure, in order to develop an increasingly well-grounded and structurally sound total system. Scientific laws and theories may be based on data obtained by means of initially adopted operational criteria, but they will not fit those data exactly; as we have seen, other considerations, including that of systematic simplicity, play an important role in the adoption of scientific hypotheses. And since the laws or theoretical principles thus accepted are then, at least tentatively, taken to express correctly the relations among the concepts that figure in them, it is not to be wondered at that the initial operational criteria come to be regarded as affording only approximate characterizations of those concepts.

Thus, empirical import as reflected in clear criteria of application, on which operationism rightly puts much emphasis, is not the only desideratum for scientific concepts: systematic import is another indispensable requirement—so much so that the empirical interpretation of theoretical concepts may be changed in the interest of enhancing the systematic power of the theoretical network. In scientific inquiry, concept formation and theory formation must go hand in hand.

7.4 On
"operationally
meaningless"
questions

One of the intriguing problems Bridgman discusses, to illustrate the critical use of operational standards, concerns the possibility of an undetectable change in the absolute scale of length. Is it not possible that all distances in the universe change steadily in such a way that they double within every 24 hours? [7] This phenomenon could never be detected by science, since the rods used in the operational determination of lengths would lengthen at the same rate. Bridgman therefore declares the question meaningless: as judged by operational standards, there would be no such universal expansion; the claim that nevertheless it might occur—unknown to us and forever undetectable by us—has simply no operational significance, no consequences testable by means of measuring operations.

This appraisal has to be changed, however, when we consider that in physics the concept of length is not used in isolation, but functions in laws and theories that link it to various other concepts. And if the hypothesis of universal expansion is combined with such other physical principles, serving as auxiliary hypotheses (cf. Chapter 3), then it does indeed yield operationally testable implications and thus is no longer meaningless. For example, if the hypothesis is true, then the time a sound signal takes to make the round trip between two points—say, on the opposite shores of a lake—should double every 24 hours; and this would be testable. But suppose we modify the hypothesis by adding the further assumption that the velocity of acoustical and electromagnetic signals increases at exactly the same rate as all distances? Then the new hypothesis would still have test implications; for example, if we assume that the universal expansion does not affect the energy output of stars such as the sun, their brightness should decrease to one-fourth of its initial value during any 24-hour period, since their surface would quadruple during that time. Thus, the fact that a hypothesis, taken in isolation, offers no possibility of operational test affords no sufficient reason for rejecting it as devoid of empirical content or as scientifically meaningless. We must, rather, consider the statement in the systematic context of the other laws and hypotheses in which it is to function, and we must examine the test implications to which it may then give rise. This procedure will by no means qualify as meaningful all hypotheses that might be proposed; among others, the hypotheses about vital forces and about universal natural affinities, discussed earlier, would still be excluded.

[7] This formulation is slightly more specific than Bridgman's (on p. 28 of *The Logic of Modern Physics*), but it involves no change in the crucial points.

Our consideration of operationism was prompted by the thought
that if a theory is to be applicable to empirical phenomena, its
characteristic terms will have to be suitably interpreted with the
help of an antecedently available, pretheoretical vocabulary. Our
discussion has shown that the operationist conception of such an
interpretation provides helpful suggestions but requires considerable mod-
ifications. In particular, we have to reject the notion that a scientific
concept is "synonymous" with a set of operations. For, first, there may
be—and there usually are—several alternative criteria of application for
a term; and these are based on different sets of operations. Second,
in order to understand the meaning of a scientific term and to use it
properly, we have to know also its systematic role, indicated by the
theoretical principles in which it functions and which connect it with
other theoretical terms. Third, a scientific term cannot be considered
"synonymous with" a set of operations in the sense of having its meaning
fully determined by them; for as we have seen, any one set of testing
operations affords criteria of application for a term only within a limited
range of conditions. Thus, the operations of using a measuring rod or
a thermometer provide only *partial interpretations* for the terms 'temperature' and 'length'; for each is applicable only within a limited range
of circumstances.

While in this respect operational criteria say less than would be
required of a full definition, there is another respect in which they say
more—indeed too much to constitute definitions in the usual understanding. Ordinarily, a stipulative definition is conceived as a sentence
that introduces a convenient term or abbreviatory symbol by simply
specifying its *meaning*—without adding any factual information. But
two operational criteria for one and the same term do have empirical
implications if, as is often the case, their ranges of application overlap.
This follows from our earlier observations about the requirement of consistency for alternative operational criteria. If different test procedures
are adopted as criteria of application for one and the same term, it follows from the statements of those criteria that in cases where more than
one of the test procedures are applicable, the procedures will yield the
same result; and this implication has the character of an empirical
generalization. The statement we considered earlier, expressing the numerical equality of "optical" and "tactual" length in all cases where
both measuring procedures can be used, is an example. Another one is
the statement that within the range where both mercury and alcohol
are liquid, the temperature readings of mercury thermometers and of
alcohol thermometers are numerically equal. This statement is a consequence of the stipulation that either kind of thermometer may be
used in the operational determination of temperatures. In sum, then,

interpretative sentences providing criteria of application for scientific terms frequently combine the stipulative function of a definition with the descriptive function of an empirical generalization.

There is yet another interesting and important respect in which interpretative sentences differ from definitions in the sense we considered earlier. Scientific terms are often used only in locutions or phrases of some characteristic form; for example, the concept of hardness as characterized by the scratch test is meant to serve only in expressions of the form 'mineral m_1 is harder than mineral m_2', and in other phrases that are definable by means of such expressions. In such cases, it is sufficient to have an interpretation for those characteristic expressions. In our example, such an interpretation is provided by the scratch test, which gives an empirical meaning to 'm_1 is harder than m_2' but not to the term 'hardness' by itself, nor to such expressions as 'mineral m is hard' or 'the hardness of mineral m is so and so much'.

Statements that fully specify the meaning of a particular context containing a given term are called *contextual definitions*, in contradistinction to so-called *explicit* definitions, such as: 'Acid' is to have the same meaning as 'electrolyte that furnishes hydrogen ions'. Analogously, we may say, then, that intepretative sentences for a scientific theory usually provide *contextual* interpretations for theoretical terms. The various ways of measuring length, for example, do not interpret the term 'length' by itself, but only such phrases as 'the length of the distance between points A and B' and 'the length of line l'; criteria for the measurement of time do not explicate the concept of time in general; and so forth. In the case of some theoretical concepts, only very special, and rather restricted, contexts may permit of an interpretation that affords a basis for experimental test. Take such terms as 'atom', 'electron', 'photon'. It is indeed possible to give a *theoretical definition* of the term 'electron', i.e., one that makes use of other theoretical terms ('electron' means 'elementary particle of rest mass 9.107×10^{-28} g, charge 4.802×10^{-10} statcoulomb, and a spin of one-half unit'); but what could an operational definition of the term be like? Surely, we cannot expect to be given operational rules for determining whether the word 'electron' applies to a given object—i.e., whether that object is an electron. What can be formulated, however, are contextual interpretations for certain kinds of statement containing the term 'electron', such as these: 'there are electrons on the surface of that insulated metal sphere'; 'electrons are escaping from this electrode'; 'this condensation track in the cloud chamber marks the path of an electron', and the like. Analogous remarks apply to the concepts of electric and magnetic field. Operational criteria can be formulated for ascertaining the structure of such fields and their strength in given areas; such criteria will refer to the behavior of probes, to the paths of particles moving in the field, to the flow of currents in wires moving through the field, and so on. But such tests will be available only for certain special, experimentally favorable kinds of field conditions, such as a homogeneous field in a sufficiently large area, or strong gradients over certain distances, or the like; a statement expressing some theoretically possible, but highly intricate field condition (involving, perhaps, strong changes over very short distances) may have no specific "operationally testable" implications.

It should now be clear that the terms of a scientific theory cannot properly be thought of as having, each, a finite number of specific operational criteria, or more generally, of interpretative statements attached to them. For interpretative statements are thought to determine ways in which sentences containing the interpreted term may be tested; i.e., when combined with such sentences, they are to yield test implications for them, couched in terms of an antecedently available vocabulary. Thus, the operational interpretation of hardness by means of the scratch test permits the derivation of test implications from sentences of the form 'm_1 is harder than m_2'; the interpretation based on the litmus test does the same for sentences of the form 'liquid l is an acid', and so forth. Now the various ways in which (or test implications by which) sentences containing the terms of a scientific theory can be tested will be determined by the bridge principles of the theory. These principles, as we noted in Chapter 6, connect the characteristic entities and processes assumed by the theory with phenomena that can be described in pretheoretical terms; and thus they link the theoretical terms to antecedently understood ones. But those principles do not assign to a theoretical term some finite number of criteria of application. Consider once more the term 'electron'. We noted that not every sentence containing this term will have definite test implications assigned to it. Yet the sentences containing the term which do yield test implications are of unlimited diversity, and the corresponding diversity of tests cannot without arbitrariness be considered as conforming to just two, or seven, or twenty different criteria of application for the term 'electron'. Here, then, the conception of the terms of a theory being individually interpreted by a finite number of operational criteria has to be abandoned in favor of the idea of a set of bridge principles that do not interpret the theoretical terms individually, but provide an indefinite variety of criteria of application by determining an equally indefinite variety of test implications for statements containing one or more of the theoretical terms.

THEORETICAL REDUCTION

8

8.1 The
mechanism-
vitalism
issue
We considered earlier the neovitalistic doctrine that certain characteristics of living systems—among them their adaptive and self-regulating features—cannot be explained by physical and chemical principles alone, but have to be accounted for by reference to new factors, of a kind not known in the physical sciences, namely entelechies or vital forces. Closer consideration showed that the concept of entelechy as used by neovitalists cannot possibly provide an explanation of any biological phenomenon. The reasons that led us to this conclusion do not, however, automatically dispose of the basic neovitalistic idea that biological systems and processes differ in certain fundamental respects from purely physico-chemical ones. This view is opposed by the so-called mechanistic claim that living organisms are nothing else than very complex physico-chemical systems (though not, as the old-fashioned term 'mechanism' would suggest, purely mechanical ones). These conflicting conceptions have been the subject of an extensive and heated debate, whose details we cannot consider here. But evidently, the issue can be fruitfully discussed only if the meaning of the opposing claims can be made sufficiently clear to show what sorts of argument and evidence can have a bearing on the problem and how the controversy might be settled. It is this characteristically philosophical problem of clarifying the meanings of the conflicting conceptions that we shall now consider; the result of our reflections will also have certain implications concerning the possibility of settling the issue.

Ostensibly, the controversy concerns the question whether or not living organisms are "merely", or exclusively, physico-chemical systems. But just what would it mean to say that they are? Our introductory remarks suggest that we might construe the doctrine of mechanism as making this twofold claim: (M_1) all the characteristics of living organisms are physico-chemical characteristics—they can be fully described in terms of the concepts of physics and chemistry; (M_2) all aspects of the behavior of living organisms that can be explained at all can be explained by means of physico-chemical laws and theories.

As for the first of these assertions, it is clear that at present, at any rate, the description of biological phenomena requires the use not only of physical and chemical terms, but of specifically biological terms that do not occur in the physico-chemical vocabulary. Take the statement that in the first stage of mitosis, there occurs, among other things, a contraction of the chromosomes in the nucleus of the dividing cell; or take the much less technical statement that a fertilized goose egg, when properly hatched, will yield a gosling. Thesis M_1 implies that the biological entities and processes here referred to—goslings, goose eggs, cells, nuclei, chromosomes, fertilization, and mitosis—can all be fully characterized in physico-chemical terms. The most plausible construal of this claim is that the corresponding biological terms, 'gosling', 'cell', etc., can be *defined* with the help of terms taken from the vocabulary of physics and chemistry. Let us refer to this more specific version of M_1 as M'_1. Similarly, if all biological phenomena—and thus, in particular, all the uniformities expressed by biological laws—are to be explainable by means of physico-chemical principles, then all the laws of biology will have to be derivable from the laws and theoretical principles of physics and chemistry. The thesis—let us call it M'_2—that this is indeed the case may be regarded as a more specific version of M_2.

Jointly, the statements M'_1 and M'_2 express what is often called the thesis of *reducibility of biology to physics and chemistry*. This thesis concerns both the concepts and the laws of the disciplines concerned: reducibility of the concepts of one discipline to those of another is construed as definability of the former in terms of the latter; reducibility of the laws is analogously construed as derivability. Mechanism may thus be said to assert the reducibility of biology to physics and chemistry. The denial of this claim is sometimes referred to as the thesis of the *autonomy of biology* or, better, of biological concepts and principles. Neovitalism thus affirms the autonomy of biology and supplements this claim with its doctrine of vital forces. Let us now consider the mechanistic theses in more detail.

8.2 Reduction of terms   The thesis M'_1 concerning the definability of biological terms is not meant, of course, to assert the possibility of assigning physico-chemical meanings to biological terms by arbitrary stipulative definitions. It takes for granted that the terms in the vocabulary of biology have definite technical meanings but claims that, in a sense we must try to clarify, their import can be adequately expressed with the help of physical and chemical concepts. The thesis, then, affirms the possibility of giving what, in Chapter 7, we broadly called "descriptive definitions" of biological concepts in physico-chemical terms. But the definitions in question could hardly be expected to be analytic. For it would obviously be false to claim that for every biological term—for example, 'goose egg', 'retina', 'mitosis', 'virus', 'hormone'—there exists an expression in physico-chemical terms that has the same meaning in the sense in which 'spouse' may be said to have the same meaning as, or to be synonymous with, 'husband or wife'. It would be very difficult to name even one biological term for which a physico-chemical synonym can be specified; and it would be preposterous to saddle mechanism with this construal of its claim. But descriptive definition may also be understood in a less stringent sense, which does not require that the definiens have the same meaning, or intension, as the definiendum, but only that it have the same extension or application. The definiens in this case specifies conditions that, as a matter of fact, are satisfied by all and only those instances to which the definiendum applies. A traditional example is the definition of 'man' by 'featherless biped'; it does not assert that the word 'man' has the same meaning as the expression 'featherless biped', but only that it has the same extension, that the term 'man' applies to all and only those things that are featherless bipeds, or that being a featherless biped is both a necessary and a sufficient condition for being a man. Statements of this kind might be referred to as *extensional definitions*; they can be schematically expressed in the form

————— has the same extension as — — —

The definitions to which a mechanist might point to illustrate and support his claim concerning biological concepts are of this extensional type: they express necessary and sufficient physico-chemical conditions for the applicability of biological terms, and they are therefore the results of often very difficult biophysical or biochemical research. This is illustrated by the characterization of substances such as penicillin, testosterone, and cholesterol in terms of their molecular structures—an achievement that permits the "definition" of the biological terms by means of purely chemical ones. But such definitions do not purport to express the *meanings* of the biological terms. The original meaning of the word 'penicillin', for example, would have to be indicated by characterizing penicillin as an antibacterial substance produced by the fungus *penicillium notatum*; testosterone is originally defined as a male sex hormone, produced by the testes; and so forth. The characterization of these substances by their molecular structure is arrived at, not by meaning analysis, but by chemical analysis; the result constitutes a biochemical discovery, not a logical or philosophical one; it is expressed by empirical laws, not by statements of synonymy. In fact, acceptance of the chemical characterizations as new definitions of the biological terms involves a change not only in meaning or intension, but also in extension. For the chemical criteria qualify as penicillin or as testosterone certain substances that were not produced by organic systems, but were synthesized in a laboratory.

At any rate, however, the establishment of such definitions requires empirical research. We must conclude therefore that, in general, the question whether a biological term is "definable" by means of physical and chemical terms alone cannot be settled by just contemplating its meaning, nor by any other nonempirical procedure. Hence, the thesis M'_1 cannot be established or refuted on *a priori* grounds, i.e., by considerations that can be developed "prior to"—or better, independently of—empirical evidence.

8.3 Reduction of laws   We turn now to the second thesis, M'_2, in our construal of mechanism—the thesis asserting that the laws and theoretical principles of biology are derivable from those of physics and chemistry. It is clear that logical deductions from statements couched exclusively in physical and chemical terms will not yield characteristically biological laws, since these have to contain also specifically biological terms.[1] To obtain such laws, we will need some additional premises that express connections between physico-chemical characteristics and biological ones. The logical situation here is the same as in the explanatory use of a theory, where bridge principles are required, in addition to internal theoretical principles, for the derivation of consequences that can be expressed exclusively in pretheoretical terms. The additional premises required for the deduction of biological laws from physico-chemical ones would have to contain both biological and physico-chemical terms and would have the character of laws connecting certain physico-chemical

---

[1] It might seem obvious that the consequences logically deducible from a set of premises cannot contain any "new" terms, i.e., terms that do not occur in the premises. But this is not so. The physical statement 'When a gas is heated under constant pressure, it expands' logically implies 'When a gas is heated under constant pressure, it expands or turns into a swarm of mosquitoes.' In this manner, then, biological statements are deducible from physical ones alone. But the same physical premiss also permits the deduction of the statements 'When a gas is heated under constant pressure, it expands or does *not* turn into a swarm of mosquitoes'; 'When a gas heated under constant pressure, it expands or turns into a rabbit', and so on. Generally, any biological statement that can be deduced from the given physical law has this peculiarity: if the specifically biological terms occurring in it are replaced by their negates or by any other terms, the sentence thus obtained is equally deducible from the physical law. In this sense, the physical law fails to offer an explanation for any specific biological phenomenon.

aspects of a phenomenon with certain biological ones. A connective statement of this kind might take the special form of the laws we have just considered, which afford a basis for an extensional definition of biological terms. Such a statement asserts, in effect, that the presence of certain physico-chemical characteristics (e.g., a substance being of such and such a molecular structure) is both necessary and sufficient for the presence of a certain biological characteristic (e.g., being testosterone). Other connective statements might express physico-chemical conditions that are necessary but not sufficient, or conditions that are sufficient but not necessary, for a given biological characteristic. The generalizations 'where there is vertebrate life there is oxygen' and 'any nerve fiber conducts electric impulses' are of the former kind; the statement that the nerve gas tabun (characterized by its molecular structure) blocks nervous activity and thus causes death in man is of the second kind. Connective statements of various other types are also conceivable.

One very simple form that the derivation of a biological law from a physico-chemical one might take can be schematically described as follows: Let 'P_1', 'P_2' be expressions containing only physico-chemical terms, and let 'B_1', 'B_2' be expressions containing one or more specifically biological terms (and possibly physico-chemical ones as well). Let the statement 'all cases of P_1 are cases of P_2' be a physico-chemical law—we will call it L_P—and let the following connecting laws be given: 'All cases of B_1 are cases of P_1' and 'All cases of P_2 are cases of B_2' (the first states that physico-chemical conditions of kind P_1 are necessary for the occurrence of the biological state or condition B_1; the second, that physico-chemical conditions P_2 are sufficient for biological feature B_2). Then, as is readily seen, a purely biological law can be logically deduced from the physico-chemical law L_P in conjunction with the connecting laws; namely, 'all cases of B_1 are cases of B_2' (or: 'Whenever the biological features B_1 occur then so do the biological features B_2').

Generally, then, the extent to which biological laws are explainable by means of physico-chemical laws depends on the extent to which suitable connecting laws can be established. And that, again, cannot be decided by *a priori* arguments; the answer can be found only by biological and biophysical research.

8.4 Mechanism restated The physical and chemical theories and the connecting laws available at present certainly do not suffice to reduce the terms and laws of biology to those of physics and chemistry. But research in the field is rapidly advancing and is steadily expanding the reach of a physico-chemical interpretation of biological phenomena. One might therefore construe mechanism as the view that in the course of further scientific research, biology will eventually come to be reduced to physics and chemistry. But this formulation calls for a word of caution. In our discussion, we have assumed that a clear distinction can be drawn between the terms of physics and chemistry on one hand and specifically biological terms on the other. And indeed, if we were presented with any scientific term currently in use, we would probably not find it difficult to decide in an intuitive fashion whether it belonged to one or to the other of those vocabularies or to neither. But it would be very difficult to formulate explicit general criteria by means of which any scientific term now in use, and also any term that might be introduced in the future, could be unequivocally assigned to the specific vocabulary of one particular discipline. Indeed, it may be impossible to give such criteria. For in the course of future research, the dividing line between biology and physics-and-chemistry may become as blurred as that between physics and chemistry has become in our time. Future theories might well be couched in novel kinds of terms functioning in comprehensive theories that afford explanations both for phenomena now called biological and for others now called physical or chemical. To the vocabulary of such a comprehensive unifying theory, the division into physico-chemical terms and biological terms might no longer be significantly applicable, and the notion of eventually reducing biology to physics and chemistry would lose its meaning.

Such a theoretical development, however, is not at hand as yet; and in the meantime, mechanism is perhaps best construed, not as a specific thesis or theory about the character of biological processes, but as a heuristic maxim, as a principle for the guidance of research. Thus understood, it enjoins the scientist to persist in the search for basic physico-chemical theories of biological phenomena rather than resign himself to the view that the concepts and principles of physics and chemistry are powerless to give an adequate account of the phenomena of life. Adherence to this maxim has certainly proved very successful in biophysical and biochemical research—a credential that cannot be matched by the vitalistic view of life.

8.5 Reduction of psychology; behaviorism

The question of reducibility has been raised also for scientific disciplines other than biology. It is of particular interest in the case of psychology, where it has a direct bearing on the famous psycho-physical problem, i.e., the question of the relationship between mind and body. A reductionist view concerning psychology holds, roughly speaking, that all psychological phenomena are basically biological or physico-chemical in character; or more precisely, that the specific terms and laws of psychology can be reduced to those of biology, chemistry, and physics. Reduction is here to be understood in the sense defined earlier, and our general comments on the subject apply also to the case of psychology. Thus, the reductive "definition" of a psychological term would require the specification of biological or physicochemical conditions that are both necessary and sufficient for the occurrence of the mental characteristic, state, or process (such as, intelligence, hunger, hallucination, dreaming) for which the term stands. And the reduction of psychological laws would require suitable connecting principles containing psychological terms as well as biological or physicochemical ones.

Some such connecting principles, expressing sufficient or necessary conditions for certain psychological states are indeed available: depriving an individual of food or drink or opportunity for rest is sufficient for the occurrence of hunger, thirst, fatigue; the administration of certain drugs is perhaps sufficient for the occurrence of hallucinations; the presence of certain nerve connections is necessary for the occurrence of certain sensations and for visual perception; proper oxygen supply to the brain is necessary for mental activity and indeed for consciousness.

One especially important class of biological or physical indicators of psychological states and events consists in the publicly observable behavior of the individual to whom those states or events are ascribed. Such behavior may be understood to include both large-scale, directly observable manifestations, such as body movements, facial expressions, blushing, verbal utterances, performance of certain tasks (as in psychological tests), and subtler responses such as changes in blood pressure and heartbeat, skin conductivity, and blood chemistry. Thus, fatigue may manifest itself in speech utterances ("I feel tired", etc.), in a decreasing rate and quality of performance at certain tasks, in yawning, and in physiological changes; certain affective and emotional processes are accompanied by changes in apparent skin resistance, as measured by "lie detectors"; the preferences and values a person holds express themselves in the way he responds when offered certain relevant choices; his beliefs, in verbal utterances that may be elicited from him, and also in the ways he acts—for example, a driver's belief that a road is closed may show itself in his taking a detour.

Certain characteristic kinds of "overt" (publicly observable) behavior that a subject in a given psychological state, or with a given psychological property, tends to manifest in appropriate "stimulus" or "test" situations are widely used in psychology as operational criteria for the presence of the psychological state or property in question. For intelligence or for introversion, the test situation might consist in presenting the subject with appropriate questionnaires; the response, in the answers the subject produces. The intensity of an animal's hunger drive will manifest itself in such behavioral features as salivation, the strength of the electric shock that the animal will take to reach food, or the amount of food it consumes. To the extent that the stimuli and the responses can be described in biological or physico-chemical terms, the resulting criteria may be said to afford partial specifications of meaning for psychological expressions in terms of the vocabularies of biology, chemistry, and physics. Though they are often referred to as operational definitions, they do not actually determine necessary and sufficient conditions for the psychological terms: the logical situation is quite similar to the one we encountered in examining the relation of biological terms to the physical and chemical vocabulary.

Behaviorism is an influential school of thought in psychology which, in all its different forms, has a basically reductionist orientation; in a more or less strict sense, it seeks to reduce discourse about psychological phenomena to discourse about behavioral phenomena. One form of behaviorism, which is especially concerned to ensure the objective public testability of psychological hypotheses and theories, insists that all psychological terms must have clearly specified criteria of application couched in behavioral terms, and that psychological hypotheses and theories must have test implications concerning publicly observable behavior. This school of thought rejects, in particular, all reliance on methods such as introspection, which can be used only by the subject himself in a phenomenalistic exploration of his mental world; and it does not admit as psychological data any of the "private" psychological phenomena—such as sensations, feelings, hopes, and fears—that introspective methods are said to reveal.

While behaviorists are agreed in their insistence on objective behavioral criteria for psychological characteristics, states, and events, they differ (or are noncommittal) on the question whether or not psychological phenomena are distinct from the corresponding, often very subtle and complex, behavioral phenomena—whether the latter are only their public manifestations, or whether psychological phenomena are, in some clear sense, identical with certain complex behavioral properties, states, or events. One recent version of behaviorism, which has exerted a strong influence on the philosophical analysis of psychological concepts, holds that psychological terms, though ostensibly referring to mental states and to processes "in the mind", serve, in effect, simply as a means of speaking about more or less intricate aspects of behavior—specifically, about propensities or dispositions to behave in characteristic ways in certain situations. On this view, to say of a person that he is intelligent is to say that he tends to act, or has a disposition to act, in certain characteristic ways; namely, in ways that we would normally qualify as intelligent action under the circumstances. To say of someone that he speaks Russian is not to say, of course, that he constantly utters Russian expressions, but that he is capable of a specific kind of behavior that shows itself in particular situations and that is generally considered characteristic of a person who understands and speaks Russian. Thinking of Vienna, being fond of jazz, being honest, being forgetful, seeing certain things, having certain wants can all be viewed in a similar way. And viewing them in this manner—so this form of behaviorism holds— disposes of the baffling aspect of the mind-body problem: there is then no point any more to searching for the "ghost in the machine",[2] for the mental entities and processes that go on "behind" the physical façade. Consider an analogy. Of a watch that keeps time very well we say that it has a very high accuracy; to ascribe high accuracy to it is tantamount to saying that it tends to keep time well. It makes no sense, therefore, to ask in what manner that nonsubstantial agency, the accuracy, acts upon the mechanism of the clock; nor does it make sense to ask what happens to the accuracy when the clock stops running. Similarly, on this version of behaviorism, it makes no sense to ask how mental events or characteristics affect the behavior of an organism.

This conception, which has contributed greatly to clarifying the role of psychological concepts, is evidently reductionist in tenor; it presents the concepts of psychology as affording an effective and convenient way of speaking about subtle patterns of behavior. The supporting arguments, however, do not establish that all the concepts of psychology are actually *definable* in terms of nonpsychological concepts of the kind required to describe overt behavior and behavioral dispositions; and this for at least two reasons. First, it is very doubtful that all the different kinds of situation in which a person could "act intelligently" (for example), and the particular kinds of action that would qualify as intelligent in each of those situations, could be encompassed in a clearcut, fully explicit definition. Second, it seems that the circumstances under which, and the manner in which, intelligence or courage or spitefulness can manifest themselves in overt behavior cannot be adequately stated in terms of a "purely behavioristic vocabulary", which might contain biological, chemical, and physical terms as well as nontechnical expressions of our everyday language, such as 'shaking one's head', 'stretching out one's hand', 'wincing', 'grimacing', 'laughing', and the like: it seems that psychological terms are needed as well to characterize the kinds of behavior patterns, or behavioral dispositions and capacities, that such terms as 'tired', 'intelligent', 'knows Russian' presumably indicate. For whether an agent's overt behavior in a given situation qualifies as intelligent, courageous, foolhardy, courteous, rude, etc., will not simply

---

[2] This phrase was coined by Gilbert Ryle, whose stimulating and influential book, *The Concept of Mind* (London: Hutchinson, 1949) develops in detail a conception of psychological phenomena and psychological locutions that is behavioristic in the sense here briefly sketched.

depend on what the facts of the situation are, but very importantly on what the agent knows or believes about the situation in which he finds himself. A man who walks unflinchingly toward a thicket where a hungry lion is crouching is not acting courageously if he does not believe (and hence does not know) that there is a lion in the thicket. Similarly, whether a person's behavior in a given situation qualifies as intelligent will depend on what he *believes* about the situation and what objectives he *wants* to attain by his action. Thus, it appears that in order to characterize the behavioral patterns, propensities, or capacities to which psychological terms refer, we need not only a suitable behavioristic vocabulary, but psychological terms as well. This consideration does not prove, of course, that a reduction of psychological terms to a behavioristic vocabulary is impossible, but it does remind us that the possibility of such a reduction has not been established by the kind of analysis we have considered.

Another discipline to which it has been thought that psychology might eventually be reduced is that of physiology, and especially neurophysiology; but again, a full reduction in the sense we specified earlier is not remotely in sight.

Questions of reducibility arise also with respect to the social sciences, particularly in connection with the doctrine of methodological individualism,[3] according to which all social phenomena should be described, analyzed, and explained in terms of the situations of the individual agents involved in them and by reference to the laws and theories concerning individual behavior. The description of an agent's "situation" would have to take into account his motives and beliefs as well as his physiological state and various biological, chemical, and physical factors in his environment. The doctrine of methodological individualism may therefore be viewed as implying the reducibility of the specific concepts and laws of the social sciences (in a broad sense, including group psychology, the theory of economic behavior, and the like) to those of individual psychology, biology, chemistry, and physics. The problems raised by this claim fall outside the scope of this book. They belong to the philosophy of the social sciences and have been mentioned here simply as a further illustration of the problem of theoretical reducibility and as an example of the many logical and methodological affinities between the natural and the social sciences.

[3] A lucid discussion of this doctrine can be found in E. Nagel, *The Structure of Science*, pp. 535-46.

For

further

reading

The list below includes only a few selected works, most of which provide, however, extensive further references to the literature in the field.

Anthologies

A. Danto and S. Morgenbesser, eds., *Philosophy of Science*. New York: Meridian Books, 1960. (Paperback.)

H. Feigl and M. Brodbeck, eds., *Readings in the Philosophy of Science*. New York: Appleton-Century-Crofts, 1953.

E. H. Madden, ed., *The Structure of Scientific Thought*. Boston: Houghton Mifflin Company, 1960.

P. P. Wiener, ed., *Readings in Philosophy of Science*. New York: Charles Scribner's Sons, 1953.

Works by individual authors

N. Campbell, *What Is Science?* New York: Dover Publications, 1952. (Paperback.) A lucid introductory account of laws, theories, explanation, and measurement.

R. Carnap, *Philosophical Foundations of Physics*, ed. Martin Gardner. New York, London: Basic Books, Inc., 1966. A fascinating introduction to a wide range of topics in the philosophy of physics, by one of the most eminent contemporary logicians and philosophers of science.

P. Caws, *The Philosophy of Science*. Princeton: D. Van Nostrand Co., 1965. A clear introductory discussion of the main logical, methodological, and philosophical aspects of scientific theorizing.

A. Grünbaum, *Philosophical Problems of Space and Time*. New York: Alfred A. Knopf, 1963. A very substantial, carefully probing, advanced work on the structure of space and time in the light of recent physical and mathematical theory.

N. R. Hanson, *Patterns of Discovery*. Cambridge, England: At the University Press, 1958. A suggestive study of the basis and function of scientific theories by reference to classical and modern particle theories in physics.

C. G. Hempel, *Aspects of Scientific Explanation and Other Essays in the Philosophy of Science*. New York: The Free Press, 1965. Includes several essays on concept formation and explanation in the natural and the social sciences and in historiography.

E. Nagel, *The Structure of Science*. New York: Harcourt, Brace & World, Inc., 1961. This outstanding work presents a thorough and illuminating systematic survey and analysis of a wide variety of methodological and philosophical problems concerning laws, theories, and modes of explanation in the natural and the social sciences and in historiography.

K. R. Popper, *The Logic of Scientific Discovery*. London: Hutchinson and Co.; New York: Basic Books, Inc., 1959. A stimulating and highly original work that deals especially with the logical structure and the test of scientific theories. Moderately advanced level. (Also in paperback.)

H. Reichenbach, *The Philosophy of Space and Time*. New York: Dover Publications, 1958. (Paperback.) A moderately technical, but very lucid examination of the nature of space and time in the light of the special and the general theory of relativity.

I. Scheffler, *The Anatomy of Inquiry*. New York: Alfred A. Knopf, 1963. An advanced analytic study of the concepts of explanation, empirical significance, and confirmation.

S. Toulmin, *The Philosophy of Science*. London: Hutchinson's University Library, 1953. A suggestive introductory book dealing especially with the character of laws and theories and with scientific determinism. (Also in paperback.)

Substantive works on physical science

Some knowledge of science, and preferably also of its history, is highly desirable for the study of problems in the philosophy of science; for advanced work in the field, such knowledge is indispensable. The following two books offer admirably lucid and substantial introductory accounts (but definitely not popularizations) of physical science, with strong emphasis on the basic concepts and methods and on their historical development.

G. Holton and D. H. D. Roller, *Foundations of Modern Physical Science*. Reading, Mass.: Addison-Wesley Publishing Co., 1958.

E. Rogers, *Physics for the Inquiring Mind*. Princeton: Princeton University Press, 1960.

INDEX

Accidental generalization, 55-58
Adams, J. C., 52
Ad hoc hypothesis, 28-30
Alston, W., 32n.
Auxiliary hypothesis, 22-25, 28, 29, 31, 97
Avenarius, R., 42

Balmer's formula, 37-38, 39, 53, 73-74, 75
Barker, S., 45n., 88n.
Because-statement, 52-53
Behaviorism, 107-110
Benzene molecule, 16
Bohr's theory of hydrogen atom, 39, 53, 73-74, 75, 83
Boyle's law, 58, 73
Brahe, Tycho, 23-24
Bridge principles, 72-75, 78, 80, 100, 104
Bridgman, P. W., 88, 90n., 91-97

Campbell, N. R., 83, 111
Carnap, R., 46, 111

Causation, 52-53
Caws, P., 111
Cepheids, 22, 33
Childbed fever, 3-8, 12, 13, 19, 22-23, 53
Classification, 13
Conant, J. B., 8n., 40n.
Concepts, scientific:
  empirical import, 96
  as knots in nomic nets, 94
  systematic import, 94-97
  vs. terms, 85
Confirmation, 8, 18, 33-46, 63-65
  and diversity of evidence, 34-36
  and precision of test, 36-37
  from prediction of "new" facts, 37-38, 77
  and probability, 45-46
  and simplicity, 40-45 (*see also* Simplicity)
  by suppport "from above", 38-40
Conjectures, 15, 21
Consistency, requirement of; *see* Operational definition
Copernican system, 23-24, 41, 70
Counterfactual conditionals, 56, 57, 66-67
Covering law, 51
Cramér, H., 62n.
Credibility (of hypotheses), 33, 45-46
  (*see also* Confirmation)
Crucial test, 25-28
Curve fitting, 14-15, 38, 41-42, 43-44

113